SELECTIONS FROM
THE DIN OF A SMITHY

THE CRAFTSMAN SERIES

Crown 8vo. Illustrated.

A series chosen for use in schools because they combine literary merit with a practical bias.

Abridged and edited by A. F. COLLINS, B.Sc.

The Wheelwright's Shop, by GEORGE STURT. 2s. 6d.

The Autobiography of James Nasmyth, Engineer. 3s. 6d.

The Bell Rock Lighthouse, by ROBERT STEVENSON. *Second impression.* 3s. 6d.

James Watt, Craftsman and Engineer, by H. W. DICKINSON. 4s. 6d.

The Din of a Smithy, by J. A. R. STEVENSON. 3s. 6d.

THE
DIN OF A SMITHY

by
J. A. R. STEVENSON

Passages selected and arranged

by

A. F. COLLINS, B.Sc.
Inspector of Handicraft and Science
Birmingham Education Authority

". . . Three sounds of increase: the lowing
of a cow in milk, the din of a smithy, the
swish of a plough."

The Triads of Ireland

CAMBRIDGE
AT THE UNIVERSITY PRESS
1936

CAMBRIDGE UNIVERSITY PRESS
Cambridge, New York, Melbourne, Madrid, Cape Town,
Singapore, São Paulo, Delhi, Mexico City

Cambridge University Press
The Edinburgh Building, Cambridge CB2 8RU, UK

Published in the United States of America by Cambridge University Press, New York

www.cambridge.org
Information on this title: www.cambridge.org/9781107610897

© Cambridge University Press 1936

First published 1936
First paperback edition 2013

A catalogue record for this publication is available from the British Library

ISBN 978-1-107-61089-7 Paperback

CONTENTS

ILLUSTRATIONS

PLATES

TEXT-FIGURES

EDITOR'S PREFACE

In my introductions to earlier volumes of "The Craftsman Series" I have commented on the fact that records of their work written by practising craftsmen appear very infrequently, nor have there been many in the past. True, many craftsmen have produced text-books of their trades, but these are for the most part very dull affairs except to those who need them for technical study. There is, therefore, excellent reason for including selections from *The Din of a Smithy* in the series, in order to bring this unusual book into a form convenient for use in educational institutions, and to introduce it to many who may not have had the opportunity of reading the original and much larger volume.

The attention given to crafts in education has in no wise lessened since the inception of "The Craftsman Series", indeed, it has continued to grow, so that nowadays few young people pass through their school life without having at some time actually practised the beginnings of a craft. Like them, the author of *The Din of a Smithy* started at the beginning, and discovered in the ancient handicraft of the smith a life's work full of satisfying interest and pleasure. In his own field, that of decorative ironwork wrought in the fine traditions of the bygone smiths, he has to-day reached a position in which few can rival him, and this account of the first few years of his progress (may it long continue!) reveals to us much of the man behind the work.

Seldom can Harrow and Cambridge have produced a man so capable of choosing his vocation in defiance of all precedent and of making such a notable contribution to the ever-dwindling supply of things of use and beauty, honestly designed and constructed so that each (as Stevenson himself says) in numberless ways bears the signature and reveals the individuality of the maker.

Of the original *The Din of a Smithy* the Rt Hon. Walter Runciman wrote: "It is as an artist that he writes, and no one can read these pages of the life which he and his men lead, enjoying themselves in the business of creation, without realising that the artist can draw satisfaction from a craft as old as history. Hand and head are well combined in this merry work."

The present volume consists of a number of passages selected from the original, and arranged in short chapters so as to form a book complete in itself. The editor's work has been limited to this selection and arrangement, together with the provision of the brief Glossary and the Index. For the rest, the text is entirely that of the author. Most of the illustrations appeared in the larger book, but three have been specially drawn by the author for this abridgement.

My task as editor would not be complete were I not to tender my thanks to Messrs Chapman and Hall, the publishers of the original book, and to the staff of the Cambridge University Press, for their help in making possible the issue of this volume. Finally I must thank the author himself. The selection and arrangement of parts of the work of a living author are not without their pitfalls for an editor, but Mr Stevenson's collaboration has made them, if not as enjoyable as work in the smithy, at least something upon which I can look back with pleasure.

A.F.C.

BIRMINGHAM
April 1936

PLATE I

THE AUTHOR

THE DIN OF A SMITHY

BY WAY OF INTRODUCTION

Not long ago that fine journal, *The Architectural Review*, contained an interesting letter. The writer of this letter deplored the fact that England is still in a man-made sense ugly. He attributed our difficulties in growing out of this to the fact that our education teaches us to be "strangers to the age we live in, and encourages us to continue building preposterous shams of the dead past". I pondered that letter and have had it in mind in writing this book.

Although a critical appreciation of past examples is necessary if you are to catch the spirit of wrought-iron design, yet this will not give you a complete understanding of iron. It may be mighty helpful; but at best it is the method of the scientist who believes that truth can be discovered by the minute examination of a vast amount of detail. It is not enough. You must come in contact with the metal.

I think it poor fun to be tied down to periods and styles. When I design a piece of ironwork I am much more ready to be guided by the possibilities and limitations of the metal as I have learned them and by the peculiarities of the site and of its environment as I see them, than by any polite consideration of the need to make a copy of some other example of ironwork. Nor will I be led into the mistake of always treating iron architecturally, for I know how seldom this is an appropriate course. The happiest examples of smithcraft are those of the twelfth, thirteenth and fourteenth centuries, when smithing was a virile craft, unencumbered by much "designing" and unprejudiced by consideration of other styles.

In the footsteps of these crafty smiths it is my ambition to follow and to cause my men to follow. When I hand a rough sketch to my foreman and tell him to "make it", he takes the little drawing to the doorway where the light is stronger, looks at it for a moment or two and all in good time translates it into black iron. He does it by the light of nature, just as I tried to design the piece by the light of nature. Well, Nature is a good mistress; she makes no mistakes. It is we who abuse her confidence by our silly attempt at intricacy.

Between these explanations I have, I think, an excuse for having written this book which tells you besides something about the way in which my smithy, starting from a humble origin, came gradually to make decorative wrought iron for all kinds of people and places.

CHAPTER I

PAYHEMBURY

The fact that a great many people are doing the wrong job and occupying the wrong niche in life is not much recognised. It will need a commission or some other kind of long-winded deputation to establish, investigate and correct the wide circumstances which forbid the average fellow from pursuing his right vocation.

I suppose that a few people diligently seek out all the possible fulfilments of that urge which they know to be latent in them; but they are rare birds. Despite the supremacy of Man and his ability to make a choice between material things, the tide of circumstances very often overpowers him. He will be prejudiced by the fact that his Aunt Jemima is a peer's daughter and insists on his going in for turf accountancy: or else he springs from a stock of tavern-keepers in whose footsteps he is expected to follow cheerfully.

And so you can look about you and discover sailormen who long for a little farm and a few pigs, cobblers and carpenters who have outstanding ability at landscape-painting, general practitioners who ought to have been comedians, butlers who could have worn My Lord Bishop's gaiters with much discretion.

In a certain Yorkshire seaport there was—and still is, I suppose—a magnificent fish shop, a palace in its own way. The owner was getting on in years and used to spend most of his time at home on the outskirts of the town. But he would descend occasionally on the "business"—partly to keep an eye on it and partly, as he expressed it, "To show them that there's none hereabouts can fillet a sole like me." One evening he said to my father, "Look at this here *splendid* business; built-up with me own hands and all ready for that son of mine to step into. And what do you think he says he wants to be?—A hartist!"

It seems odd, therefore, that everyone should be so specialised in his own line, when you consider the chance way in which he comes to it. But this is a fact: if you want to know something of the technique of whelk-picking, or why large hairy spiders run across the drawing-room carpet in October, or why your wireless set will only emit abdominal noises, when you want it to give you the nine o'clock time signal, you must consult an expert. But this expert will know nothing about the rate of exchange, marks/pounds English, or what a knife machine looks like when you dismember it. (A fascinating thing, like the inside of a cow.) There are too many subjects nowadays—that is what it amounts to—for anyone to set up as being generally knowledgeable;

so that General Knowledge has ceased to exist except in prep.-school examinations, where it is still administered as an antidote to the effects of the Latin grammar paper.

Like everyone else I am a specialist. I specialise in the designing and making of decorative wrought-iron work. It is, I suppose, an unusual occupation; but mightily intriguing. I came to it in a roundabout way, and if it had not been for my having the wisest and kindest father and mother that a young man could have I might never have discovered it at all. But they let me look here and there, encouraging me to do any job which took my fancy: so that I finally came to the work that I like best in the world. On which account I am a very happy person and much to be envied.

I was going on to describe my smithy, to tell you of the way in which it lies in the shelter of oaks and firs and chestnut trees in Straightway Head woods; of the three Roman roads that make a triangle about it and of the golden half-guinea piece of George II, which we found when we were digging for the foundations of the place. I would like to tell you about the grey rolling moors which we can see when we stand in the doorway; and how the cock pheasants put up a mighty shouting at dusk in the autumn time when they go to roost in the trees, close to where we forge the black iron.

Because this is a book on the subject of decorative wrought-iron work I will spare you a long account of the different jobs which I performed between leaving Harrow in 1919 and making up my mind to go to New Zealand in 1926. Now I would settle down, happy thought, in New Zealand and be a farmer. Waiting for the ship which was to take me there I employed the spare time in apprenticing myself to the blacksmith at Payhembury, where I learned to shoe horses. I thought that this would be useful to me in the new country to which I was going.

The way in which exciting things have their happening is casual; an inclination towards learning to shoe horses, and out of this came "The Devon Smithy".

I'll not easily forget the circumstances which led to my learning to hammer iron in that country forge, beginning with the thrill of pleasure that went through me as I first clapt eyes on the Tale-brook, where it runs close to Donald Granger's mill. It is a gay and lovely place: you come on it by a decent road from Talaton on the one side and by a jungly lane from Payhembury village on the other.

I had found the place in the early summer of 1924; it was such a charming spot and so free that I stayed to make friends with the miller. When I said goodnight that evening I vowed that I would go there again. So I did. I went several times to Tuck Mill in the summer of 1925, to fish the Tale-brook and to take tea with the Grangers.

In 1926, when I was casting round for a smithy at which to apprentice myself, my thoughts were already on the mill and I wondered whether I could get the necessary schooling either at Payhembury or at Talaton, neither of which is more than a mile or two from the mill. I went to Payhembury on a wild February day in 1926 and broached the matter to the old blacksmith. A kindly chap: he gave me a searching look to see whether I was in earnest and then agreed. I would come at 8 a.m. of a morning, return to the mill for dinner in the middle of the day, go to the smithy again in the afternoon and so home to the mill to sleep. It was good. I took up my quarters at the mill a week later.

It had been a mere passing notion that I should apprentice myself in this way whilst waiting for my ship. I did not look on it at the time as being more than a temporary arrangement. Nevertheless the work interested me very much indeed and I used to be up early at Tuck Mill of a morning. And after breakfast away I would go up the road, the dew-spangle in the hedges and a choir of birds opening their little hearts to a new day. It was a royal existence.

And so I would come presently to the forge itself. A dark place this, and a pagan one. It is old—six hundred years, they say. It may be older still, for they say in the village that Cynewulf's dirty rabble

passed here, flying from the Saxons after the bloody
battle that was fought at Parfitt Water, half a mile
away.

They say besides that Monmouth's men came by—
what was left of them, poor lads—after Sedgemoor;
bitter, disillusioned men. And I met one old man—
he has gone his way—who swore that Elizabeth's
messengers stopped at the smithy itself on a certain
July day in the year 1588; they were bustling west-
ward to Plymouth, to Drake, bearing the Queen's
word that the little ships of England should go up
against King Philip's Armada.

All of this or a part of it or none of it may be true; but
the place is old enough. The tools of bygone smiths,
ancestors of the old 'un, litter the floor and walls
and benches: great-bellied spiders, the real inheritors
of the place, haunt the window crannies with gloomy
purpose, and the atmosphere of the forge is impreg-
nated with the dark spirit of this oldest of all the old
crafts. When the hearth fire was lighted and the old
'un stood gauntly, his body hidden in a swirling
smoky mantle, his head transfigured by the leaping
hearth-flames, I used to feel that I was novice at
some sacrificial rite or making communion with the
dark gods.

The old 'un received me with that polite incurious-
ness which hall-marks the gentleman. He asked very
few questions and he told no tales; but the rest of the
village was mightily intrigued.

Well, there in that old smithy at Payhembury I sweated and learned. My jobs were mainly shoeing ones, and I used to enjoy the smell of the pungent smoke which comes out of a burning hoof, mingled with the flat alkaline flavour of the shoeing stall. I believe that I gained a light touch: for once, when I was rasping her hoof, a mare tried to fall asleep on my shoulder and I barely escaped destruction.

Occasionally we would mend a farm implement; and when there was time to spare we would be at shoe-making for stock or mending Farmer Smale's chain-harrow. That chain-harrow never did seem to get finished. Between these occupations I would conduct a few experiments with iron, on my own account. I would make pokers and tongs, shovels and such-like trifles; and gradually it grew clear in me that I liked iron and the working of iron. I went on with my experiments, and became more certain. Thereafter my ideas about New Zealand underwent a change. And not long after this I began to look about for a smithy of my own.

I didn't know anything about iron in those days. It hadn't occurred to me to see anything more in blacksmithing than the shoeing of horses and the making of odds and ends of pokers and tongs and such. But I knew well enough that I liked the feel of iron and the excitement of whipping it bright and sparkling out of the fire; and that I liked the feel of a great horse, when his leg was under my arm—the way that he quivered at first and then relaxed his muscles as he discovered that I meant well by him.

I felt an urge to go deeply into this business; and with the help of my dear father I was able to do so and set about looking for a forge which I could call my own.

CHAPTER II

WEST HILL: THE FIRST GATE

It was a mild June day when I first came on my motor-bicycle between the fir trees, flanking the long hill which leads downhill from Prickly Pear to Ottery St Mary. I had travelled three parts of a mile when the bell-like notes of an anvil came floating on the air: they held a stirring quality of promise and encouragement. The sound of a hammer on an anvil always moves something—I don't know what it is—which is latent and fundamental in me. Perhaps it reminds me of the pact between nature and man productive—a great, gay, purposeful sound; so that I quicken my pace and hurry forward, anxious to catch the sound before it fades, as though it were some mightily important personage whom I must meet at all cost. But I write of the sound as you hear it in the country, companion to the rustle of leaves and the hushed lilt of birds twittering with the mellow orchestra of a farmyard in the distance. The anvils of a city factory are a different thing. They are cold and bleak; they pledge you man productive; but they are sorrowful. They speak of wretched, unhealthy conditions and their sound embarrasses. You must hear it in a country place if you are to discover its fine qualities.

I halted for a minute: it was an occasion important

enough, on looking back at it, to be called a crisis in my life. Then I proceeded down the hill on my motor-bicycle and discovered a little red-brick post office. There I left the bicycle and followed the sound of the hammer and came up a side lane to the smithy.

A puff of blue smoke stood away from the chimney stack and dispersed itself into the clear air in front

West Hill Smithy

of pine trees. The iron gate was open. I went up the path and looked through the smithy doorway where I found a friendly old person forging a shoe. It was Harry Potter. Whilst he finished the shoe and spiked the nail-holes I leaned against the wall and watched him and passed the time of day with the farm boy who stood at the head of the bony mare. Presently

the job was done and the mare led forth into the
sunlight, round the corner and up the hill. It was
exciting and stirring: I saw that I had done wisely
in wishing to work iron. Was it to be the outcome
of my "urge"? If so, why shouldn't this be my
smithy?

There was little beating about the bush. By a
simple transaction, sealed with a tankard of cider
apiece, the smithy became my property and Harry
Potter stayed on to work for me—a heart of gold;
he bore well with the strange notions and unusual
conceits which I began to evolve. And I christened
my forge "The Devon Smithy", and wished luck
on the place.

Even now I had no real leanings towards the
making of decorative wrought-iron work. The "connection" of the forge under old Harry had been the
shoeing of twenty-five or thirty horses with the
mending of odds and ends of wheelbarrows and the
like, the sharpening of picks and adjusting of farm
implements and an occasional frivolity in the making
of steel tips for country boot heels. Once a gypsy
child brought me a kettle to mend, and on another
occasion I healed a dog kennel of a leaky roof and
charged 1s. 3d. for this service. Rarely, very pains-
takingly, I would make up a set of fire-irons and
would sell them for a few shillings. But for the most
part it was shoeing all day long; making four shoes
and fitting them for 7s. 6d., with a chance of a kick

in the ribs which cost nothing. Try it for yourself, and see how much profit you make.

But I still pushed on with my experimenting. I got to know quite a bit about wrought iron. I discovered for example that there was a difference between iron which had been tortured into shape and iron which just flowed naturally and reasonably to its destination. I began to wonder whether I couldn't put these discoveries to some use, to find people who would buy decorative ironwork from me. It was more diversified and much more interesting than shoeing horses. Growing venturesome I began to put together a few door-latches and a trivet or two.

My first real commission for decorative ironwork took the form of an order for fire-dogs, poker and tongs for Mr C. B. Bone, of Budleigh Salterton; I can remember the excitement of getting that order and of getting paid for it.

That commission was the forerunner of one or two more of the same kind from other good friends in Salterton. I made a gate-latch and another pair of dogs and some odds and ends. And at about this time, so I see from an old ledger, we repaired a lock for Mr Perry, the parson, and charged him a shilling.

Now this tinkering with "fancy bits and pieces", as they called it, didn't meet with the approval of my worthy clientele of farmers. I remember when one of them brought his horrible, ill-tempered horse to the smithy and found me putting the finishing touches to the gate-latch about which I told you. He looked disparagingly at me and my work and then suggested that, "I did ought to stick to shoeing and not to worry myself with such-like things." I gave him something to go on with, however. For three minutes, I'm sorry to say, I abused him and told him that if it wasn't for the likes of him, expecting something for nothing, I wouldn't need to take to decorative ironworking.

That incident was by the way of being a turning-point in my career. Thenceforward I was resolved to cut myself adrift from the shoeing business and to build up a reputation for the other, more interesting, work.

It is a significant thing when you, the maker, are pleased with your work. You have lived alongside it for days or weeks or months, perhaps. You have come to know all about it; it is an open book which you alone can read clearly. Quite apart from what your customer thinks, it is a real measure of the excellence of the thing that you are pleased with it.

During the summer of 1926, we shod a great many horses, mended the water-pump of a steam roller, set one or two saw blades, sharpened a number of picks for the roadmenders who were conducting operations in the lane outside the smithy, and performed many other odd jobs. I see from my first ledger that on August 6th we mended a perambulator.

Don't think that I am making fun of these early commissions at "The Devon Smithy". I was very glad to get the work. I charged 3s. 6d. for that job

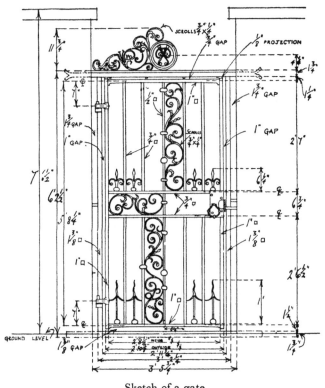

Sketch of a gate

and it was good value for the money. The opportunity to do odd jobs is not given to everyone: it is of priceless value, for it gives you an insight into workshop technique and an especial kind of re-

PLATE II

THE FIRST GATE

sourcefulness which are more precious than pearls. It is a grand thing to be independent of anyone else's hands in dealing with these twopenny-halfpenny jobs.

It is well known that important things happen always in a most unimportant way. One August morning in 1926—I forget the exact date, but it was not earlier than the 6th—someone came to the smithy and remarked to me that there was a fine wrought-iron gate outside the office of Mr Snow in Cathedral Close, Exeter. We were not very busy that morning. We had made a few shoes and I had sharpened a pick which had been brought in to me on the previous evening just before we shut down for the night. Apart from the need to make a few more shoes for stock it seemed a shame to be indoors on a lovely morning like this: so I put on my hat and jumped on my motor-bicycle and went off to see this gate for myself, leaving Harry Potter to mind the forge and to sit at the receipt of custom. Arrived at Exeter I paid a call on the owner of the gate and he very kindly gave me permission to look at it and to make a sketch of it. As I was leaving he told me that one of his clients, Mr Atherton Byrom, was anxious to find someone to make a copy of it on a smaller scale, to be fixed in the wall of the kitchen garden at Culver. I wrote to Mr Byrom and he wrote to me and, I think, came to see me: in one way and another that is how I got the order for my first gate.

The whole gate needed to be redesigned as the opening in the wall, which it was to fill, was narrow. It was impressed on me that I must keep the same effect at all costs. This meant that I should have to be very careful about the design of the "overthrow" which is the first part of a gate to catch the eye.

I enjoyed making that gate: coming my way it had been a great piece of luck. It put Harry and me on our mettle as we had never contemplated anything so ambitious as this, with the result that I had to make many discoveries for myself when we set to work on it.

For the outer frame we picked good straight bars of $1\frac{1}{2} \times 1\frac{1}{2}$ in. iron. The two verticals are spilled, top and bottom, where they pass through the top and bottom horizontals. These holes in the horizontals were punched whilst the bars were hot—a usual practice, though I am not very keen on doing this nowadays.

It was a week or two before Harry and I could get to work on it and several weeks more before we got it finished. But it was completed at last and painted; and I felt mighty proud and happy when I saw it fixed and working smoothly at Culver. Then I went back to the smithy: there was a fat cheque in my trouser pocket and shoeing had entirely lost its charm; I wondered to myself how I could ever again be satisfied with it and I speculated as to when the next order for a gate would come my way.

In September, however, we were commissioned by Mrs Fulton of Budleigh Salterton to make a pair of door-canopy brackets for her house.

Brackets are difficult to design: they consist of

A bracket

three principal parts: the vertical part (against the wall), the base or support (horizontal), and the truss. The essence of the idea is that the truss shall be straight from heel to toe, for if it departs from this the bracket will be weakened. Take a pencil and try for yourself. I will say no more here, for I want to describe some of the decorative ironwork which we made at West Hill in 1927.

April did not bring me very many orders for decorative ironwork: we were busy with the farmers' horses, making four shoes and fixing them for 7s. 6d. a time. Hard work, my masters. Nevertheless, I found time to forge a few pieces, small lanterns and a bell-pull or two.

These kept us going until May, when Mrs Washington of Dawlish commissioned me to make a simple little gate for her.

There was something of an object lesson in this gate; it convinced me of a thing which I had suspected even at this early stage of "The Devon Smithy's" history, that simple things can often be mightily decorative. Starting at this point I used to wonder why it always seemed to be more difficult to design simply than to design complicatedly. I couldn't get beyond this stage of the problem for I wasn't in a position to argue the pros and cons of the case. Later I learned many other things which took the argument into deeper water; but of these I shall speak presently.

In July, I think, we made an iron field gate, a not very convincing affair. For some reason or other the eye prefers to see the long axis of a rectangle placed vertically rather than horizontally. In a field gate the reverse is the case, a fact which always troubles me when I first set eyes on one. It is only its age-old association with timber which makes it tolerable. Iron has no place in a design of this sort.

In October 1927 the state of business was much improved; so I invested a little money in a second-hand electric lighting plant, bought from some people nearby. The installation of this little plant was a great help to me. Hitherto we had put up with oil lamps; by their meagre light it was difficult to work carefully after dark. This first lighting plant served me well until December 1928, when I bought a bigger one, a 1500 watt Kohler which at the time of writing[1] is still working for me.

[1] Written in 1932.

CHAPTER III

DEMOCRACY AND ART: UTILITY
AND ORNAMENT

Early in 1927 I made an extension to the smithy, adding a new shop and a small office which were useful and impressive. Now I had much more space in which to work and I could contemplate more happily the prospect of getting orders for big jobs-of-work of which there seemed now to be a good chance. In November, 1927, we made a wooden gate with wrought-iron fittings—hinges and latch and an open grille in the top—to the order of a certain lady who lived not a dozen miles from my smithy. This commission led unfortunately to a difference of opinion, when, in the fastness of the old person's stronghold, fierce words flew to and fro like bullets and with no less velocity. The trouble arose through my having failed to have her instructions in black and white; with the result that when the job was done she proclaimed that not only was it entirely different from what she had been led to expect, but that the sight of it gave her the ache—and so forth.

I was younger and more violent and much less tactful than (I hope) I am nowadays. I was so convinced that I was in the right about this argument that I forgot to soothe her. I have no doubt at all that I was most irritating at the time. At the same time it was a good gate and we had made an excellent job of it.

Arguments about Art never reach a satisfactory objective. This is not surprising, considering our democratic system whereby things are so arranged that anybody's opinion is as good as anyone else's. It is most difficult to establish facts or to formulate criteria of any save the material things of this earthly existence.

At one time when I was living in London I used to lodge with an old person of the name of Mrs Figgis. For a small sum I occupied a bedroom and the "front room". That front room was decorated in a style which would have brought tears of gratitude to the nineteenth century.

There was a full-blown aspidistra in the window; there were heavily embroidered antimacassars, voluptuously curved hair sofas and chairs, and china cats on the mantelpiece. And, need I tell you, a large case of pessimistic-looking canaries floated on the wall midway between floor and ceiling. The whole room was so genteel that I wanted to scream for help and to commit an act of frightfulness every time I set foot inside it. The canaries were particularly offensive to me; but Mrs Figgis set great store by them. She thought that they were lovely and artistic and I suppose that in a sense they were; they did much, I know, to soften the old person's existence in a cruel world, like the tender passages in band music. Alack-a-day; Mrs Figgis has been gathered in and I am left to lament the poor old soul and to wonder whether St Francis has taken her under his wing. She was, of course, a most worthy citizen, a highly respected member of society, and evidently knew what she was talking about. We are not in a position to contradict people of her standing; we must take refuge in the consolation that we are Superior Folk, that we "know better" than she does. And you may go forth on your daily round and meet a host of Mrs Figgises, and another host of us "knowing" ones.

This looseness of authority has a deep-seated cause. Once upon a time, not so long ago, Art was of two kinds. There was the art of the craftsman and of his patron, bringing forth from a union of nicety and cunning a thing of beauty fit for the delectation of princes and potentates, persons of wealth, leisure and culture. These patrons were the connoisseurs of their age. The other kind of Art was that of the simple, uneducated (and therefore unsophisticated) ordinary fellow, following his calling and combining steady hand with crafty eye to overcome the day's work and to put out something which would be strong and lasting. Examples of this kind of art are not ponderable until they have been tested by a probationary period of obscurity on or in the earth, coming finally to light for the speculative

verdict of another generation. I often wonder
whether a future generation will dig in the ground
and find the tin cans and bicycle tyres and broken
bedsteads of the twentieth century, to hail them as
masterpieces of a virile age!

Most of the patron-connoisseurs are gone; mass
production has ruined them as it has ruined simple
craftsmanship.

Nowadays the mass producer turns out thousands
upon thousand replicas of the original design, which
thus ceases to be unique. It has no singularity, no
personal element identifying it with some particular
maker. It is an awful thing to contemplate—the
reduction of craftsmanship to the level of a serial-
number!

Yet underneath this there runs a fine motive in
places. It appears in all kinds of art-form. It comes
to light in literature and in architecture, and even—
wonder of wonders!—in the products of the mass
producer. It takes the shape of an earnest wish to
simplify things. If she can rid herself of the complexity
of *added ornament* this will be the biggest step which
Art will have made.

In the meantime it seems to me that there are in
a general sense three categories in Art: the Art
which is useful, the Art which is decorative and that
which combines the two. I assume that any Art
object which falls perfectly into one of these categories may claim to be well designed. It is easy to

think of examples to illustrate these divisions. There are few more perfect spectacles than that of a full-rigged ship, rare in these days of steam and crude oil, as she ploughs the green water in her course and throws it aside and astern in a wide field of furrows. She is a joyful thing, and poets the world over in every age have caught the picture and have given us their conception of the tall ship.

But that ship is strictly utilitarian. Not a part of her, save for her solemn figure-head, was designed for anything beyond efficiency, whether this might be in cargo capacity or in swiftness through the sea. Not a splinter nor a strand of her was designed to be decorative. Through her capacity to do her job well and truly she is seen to be supremely well designed.

It is easy to think of other objects which solely on account of their utility are well designed—farm wagons and the homely spade and other kinds of tools. I never come out of a cobbler's shop without pleasure from the strong, shiny instruments of his craft. In fact most tools are supremely well designed, being full of artistic merit, despite their making no pretensions to be decorative. They fit the hand.

There are not many objects of the second order, those whose function is to be decorative. But such things as pictures and pieces of sculpture (and cases of stuffed canaries) belong to this category. These make no claim to be useful, their justification lying in the measure in which they please the eye, this being determined by the rather vague process of referring them to fashion or to a connoisseur. It is this lack of utility which makes it so hard for anyone to judge them. For the fact is that anyone can tell you whether a spade will do its job, provided that he is clever enough to know which is the proper end to put in the ground.

By far the most numerous are those of the third category, combining utility with decoration. Their name is legion, and I will not trouble you with a list of all the chairs and tables, clothes, motor-cars and buildings and a million-and-one other sorts of man-made objects which combine usefulness with decoration. In most cases the objects in this class were designed purely for utility, only that the designer thought that they would be more agreeable if they had a few twiddles. Ah, there is a key to the whole matter: twiddling is a sore temptation, and your designer finds nothing easier than to overlay, to encrust or "enrich" the dull, utilitarian parts of his design. Why is this? There is a very simple explanation: *Designers are no longer responsible for making things: they only "design" them.*

In the old days the designer was also the maker; those charming (but insanitary) Elizabethan cottages were mostly designed by their builders. If this was not the case, their designer was more than capable of laying a brick or of using a cross-saw. How many architects climb the scaffolding nowadays and how many of these can take the tool from the workman's hand and show him how to do the job? Designing as a separate craft is quite a recent innovation, having attained to recognition at the Renaissance, more or less. The very word "architect" meant— in the Greek—"a master builder".

No one admires the architectural profession more than I do; they are sterling people and the field of their knowledge and experience is immense; yet you must appreciate the fact that times without number the craftsman is asked by the architect to carry out work which obviously can't be done (or which shouldn't be done).

Under mass production it seems to be inevitable that the design staff should be in a separate compartment from that of the manufacturing staff. Any of my readers who have visited the works of a big industrial concern must have been struck by this cleavage, by the rather snobbish regard towards the "hands" on the part of the drawing office and no less by the contemptuous attitude of the workshop towards the "pencil-pushers" upstairs.

This is an ancient controversy; the designer always thinks that he knows better than the craftsman. And in a sense he may be forgiven for taking the attitude that it is the duty of the shop to see that his designs are carried out exactly. Unhappily, it often happens that the design is structurally im-

possible, but it needs the maker to see this and to
point it out to its reluctant author! If the designer
had known a little more about the way in which
things are put together the difficulty would never
have arisen.

At this moment, sad to relate, a million designers
are sitting on their little stools plying their pencils.
They are beyond doubt worthy citizens and hard-
working chaps. But they are no exception to a
general rule. *They are all trying desperately hard to be
clever: they have forgotten the value of simple things.* Man's
mass-need has put those designers in the place which
they occupy and has let them loose in a long-suffer-
ing world. They are free to commit every extrava-
gance of intricacy, care-free and unassailable. Who-
soever criticises them is a voice crying in the wilder-
ness, for they seem incapable of learning that it needs
genius to design simply. I have talked to many
draughtsmen about this, and the discussion terminates
nearly always in the same way; they cannot fathom
that sort of simplicity which has no recourse to the
camouflage of ornament. They have forgotten that
any and every design must depend on the old, wise,
fundamental principles of mass, proportion, texture
and colour; that it must bulk rightly; that every
part of it must contrast sympathetically with every
other part.

Analyse that sailing ship of which I wrote and you
will discover that these four principles are the secrets

of her loveliness and the whole explanation of her utility. Those cobbler's tools, when you get past the mere pleasure which they give you and begin to analyse them, are seen to be supremely well proportioned. It is the measure of all good tools.

The other day a large and overbearing woman came to my smithy and into my office. When I showed her my designs she sniffed and made disparaging remarks. Then she said, "But they're too *simple*! They're not nearly elaborate enough."

If this expresses our outlook we must not be surprised that designers have followed ornamental rather than utilitarian designs.

Happily for me the work which began to flow towards "The Devon Smithy" enabled me to put some of these ideas into practice. I didn't want to be entirely constrained in the matter of keeping my designs on a simple basis: but a year's handling of wrought iron had convinced me that in order to get the best results I must not try to be "clever" with it. This might (and probably it actually did) eliminate a number of designs which were superficially quite jolly and intriguing to the casual sense. Nevertheless I was convinced that I was working on the right lines, and that if the idea was unattainable (or undesirable) the exercise was a good one and would at least prevent my taking unwarrantable liberties with the black iron.

CHAPTER IV

THE DESIGN OF DECORATIVE
WROUGHT-IRON WORK

Very little investigation will be needed to convince yourself that wrought iron falls into the category of "useful" things. It is a hard, dark, dour thing. Ffoulkes in his book[1] quotes the Monk of St Gall, whose account of the equipage of Charlemagne catches the spirit of the stuff. "The fields and open places were filled with iron....The horror of the dungeon seemed less than the bright gleam of the iron. 'Oh the iron, woe for the iron!' was the cry of the citizens. The strong walls shook at the sight of iron, the resolution of old and young fell before the iron."

In an earlier part of the same book, Ffoulkes makes the assertion: "Of all the crafts which have been the outcome of the development and civilisation of man, either for practical or for decorative purposes, none has exercised such an important influence as that of the Smith...for the whole foundation of civilised life, all its necessities, comforts, conveniences, and pleasures from the earliest times up to the present day owe their very existence in the first place to the Man at the Anvil...."

[1] *Decorative Ironwork*, by Charles Ffoulkes.

There is a positiveness about this which may be questioned. But the smallest investigation will show that the claim is no exaggerated one. The carpenter must call in the smith to make and set his tools and so must the builder and stone carver; the goldsmith and jeweller are alike indebted to him. The dependence of mankind on this humble fellow cannot be exaggerated; the most casual reflection will show its truth.

But these touch only the man whose craft it is to alter the shape of wrought iron. Of themselves, they do not embrace the utilitarian importance of the part which his iron (and steel, its close ally) play in human activities. If we consider the place which the two metals occupy in railways, shipping and other forms of transport and in the making of tools for all sorts and kinds of manufactures and professions we can revise our idea of the humble fellow and his smoky forge, all beneath the spreading chestnut tree: we must recognise in him a quality of supreme indispensability. Civilisation is rooted in his craft: he is a high covenant in that contract between Man and his fellow men, which we call by the name of "society".

It follows therefore that if ironwork perfectly fulfils a useful function it may claim—like the sailing ship—to be "well designed". The very best examples of wrought-iron work have exhibited this sheer utilitarianism and freedom, partial or complete, from

PLATE III

THE DEVON SMITHY

added ornament. I know nothing much of other materials; but I am quite certain that any attempt to be "clever" or "exuberant" with iron is contrary to its nature and to its useful function, and that it is therefore fatal to its good design. The metal must be made to speak its decorative quality—and will readily do so—through mass, proportion and texture; in these terms the piece will be coherent. Mere ornament added as an after-thought will be meaningless, as is much wrought-iron work of to-day, consisting—as it does—in a mass of ornament superimposed on a bare structure. This may seem to be a counsel of perfection. But even if it is unattainable the contemplation of it is a good exercise. The structure of the finished piece should be decorative in itself, in such a fashion that it will not need the addition of ornament. If you must add ornament, discover how much you need rather than how much you can use. And if you are so wise that you know how to merge structure and ornament into an undifferentiable whole then you will have achieved a perfect example of wrought-iron work, and people should point you out to their friends when you pass by in the street.

But even in the halcyon days of ironwork, in the twelfth, thirteenth and fourteenth centuries, there must have been a temptation to complicate things. That old smith, at work on the hinges for the treasury doors, found himself tempted towards a flourish or two, supplementary to the pure utility of the piece. I expect that he looked out innocently from his forge-side, to find his gaze checked by the blackthorn trees growing opposite the smithy, bright with their load of blossom and all a-quiver in the country breeze. He must have longed to make a copy of it and to add a twiddle or two on his own account. Because he was an old and crafty one, full of a knowledge of what iron could do and of what it could not do and steeped in the pagan, elemental rites of his hearth-side those twiddles of his are good to look upon, as we all know.

When I am in London I sometimes pass through a squalid area—Soho, to be precise—where men and women toil miserably in half-underground work-shops, their heads on a level with the boots of passers-by, working out their lives in conditions too awful to be contemplated. Dust and dirt and cheese-like complexions; what a price the town-dweller seems to pay for his shops and theatres, for his libraries and galleries.

As the years go by and "The Devon Smithy" grows up, I am more than ever convinced that the countryside really is the proper place for ironworking. This is neither sentiment nor prejudice: smithing is fundamentally a thing of England's country places.

If you will follow my advice and apprentice your-self to a village forge you will soon be convinced that what I say is true: you need to have your eyes and ears full of country sights and sounds and your nose full of country smells, if you are to reach the foundations of this old craft.

Get you down into some country smithy or other and wear an apron and a shirt open at the neck. If you have never drawn a bar of iron golden and sparkly from the hearth fire, to slap it down on the anvil and to bang it into shape with great, over-arm blows of your hammer, you've missed one of the solid pleasures. Away fly the sparks across the smithy and through the doorway: your throat parches, your feet tingle and you feel light and airy and strangely untired. But go warily and piously, for you practise the unchanging craft that was ancient when Tubal-cain taught it to his followers long ago. So that when the night comes, drawing the long shadows from their hiding-places in corner and cranny, at just that pregnant hour between the fulfilment of night and the passing of day you, smith, have won through to another plane and not all the priests of church shall break your covenant with the spirit of your hearth-side.

At my smithy we work principally from my own drawings and designs; but very often we are asked to make ironwork to other people's ideas and then the drawings are given to us. They are sometimes most beautiful examples of composition and draughtsmanship with every detail carefully scheduled, leaving us free to go ahead with the work and saving

3-2

us a certain amount of trouble. But now and then we get a drawing which is impossible to interpret! It makes ridiculous demands both of ourselves and of the iron. Then we have to set about doing as well as we can and when the piece is finished, we are seldom pleased with it. Let me describe, on the other hand, the way in which we make drawings for ourselves.

In the early days of the smithy before we began to make big pieces of ironwork I never bothered myself about carefully measured drawings. I used first to design the idea in charcoal and then in pencil, finally expanding this pencil sketch to show the general measurements of the thing, including the site which it was to occupy. A visitor would come to the smithy and would tell me that he had a gateway in a brick wall 8 ft. 6 in. high, between brick, stone-capped piers 4 ft. o in. apart; and would I design a gate for it? If the site was accessible I would visit the place and make a charcoal sketch of it, developing this when I got back to the smithy.

Alternatively, my enquirer would send me a photograph containing one or two of the principal measurements and a few remarks on materials, colour, texture and so on. From this information I would make in duplicate a coloured sketch, showing the proposed gate located in its proper site. The sketch would usually be made to an inch/foot scale. One of the two copies would go to my customer for approval and the second one would be retained at the smithy. And supposing that I was given word to go ahead with the work, the next step would be a consultation between myself and my foreman as to the most suitable iron to be used in the job. After one or two small amendments to the sketch a very simple working drawing would be attached and sent with it to the shop for the work to be carried out.

Now a sketch—more particularly a coloured one—is of priceless value not only to your customers but also to the workshop. A good many ironworking firms make it a practice to send out elaborate blueprints by way of illustrating the design. These are all very well in their way of representing a draughtsman's idea of the design. But the average lay person cannot read a drawing of this sort; and besides, this wrought-iron work does not lend itself to much draughtsmanship. It is most difficult to represent it in two dimensions. It is the *impression* of the stuff which you must catch by means of a sketch, and then put the work into the hands of some crafty smith who can translate the idea with feeling and understanding. All this sounds rather vague; but I assure you that it is a course which produces good results.

Thereafter it is the task of the smith to address himself in person to the work before him. The more he can keep the job in his own hands without letting apprentice boys and improvers take a share in it, the more surely will the finished piece reflect his personality and care and love which he has bestowed on it. This is where pre-Renaissance ironwork is so jolly and sincere, a thing which cannot always be said of the work of the later masters. That old stuff simply glows with the personality of the smith who made it; you can see this in the little errors and blemishes and irregularities which make pleasant variance along the surface of the piece. To say that these old craftsmen understood how to manage these things is a wrong term, for the act was instinctive and unselfconscious, and remained so until the Renaissance with its stimulus to abstract ideas brought a final cleavage between design and manufacture. They were unspoiled, these old 'uns; unhampered by considerations of being "clever"; unhindered in their sympathetic understanding of iron by the foibles of other people's ideas. If you wish to emulate them I recommend you to use as few drawings as need be. A comprehensive sketch and one or two principal measurements—and for the rest there are many crafty smiths in old England who can put their own interpretations on that sketch of yours and turn out a very good job on their own account.

CHAPTER V

HAMMER AND IRON

If you go down to a smithy and hammer iron for yourself you will soon discover that it gives the best

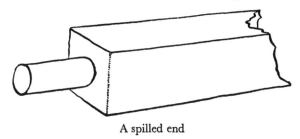

A spilled end

results when you avoid cutting it. Iron isn't like brick or stone or wood (though I do not profess to be expert about these). To treat it sympathetically you

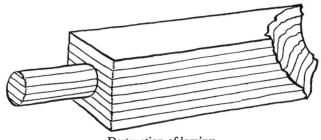

Destruction of laminæ

must get it hot and *push it into shape with a hammer.* Iron is a *laminated* material; if you cut through these laminæ you destroy some of them. A practical example of this, often encountered in the smithy, lies in the various ways in which you can make a "spilled end". There are two ways of making such a spilled end. Suppose that you want to make one on the end of a 1 in. × 1 in. bar; you can if you like put the bar through the headstock of a lathe and turn down the spill with a cutting-tool. This will make a beautiful, smoothly finished job of the work. Yet this process will have done irreparable damage to the bar; you will have cut through the laminæ.

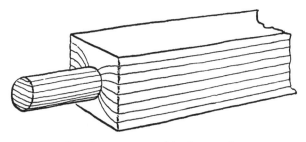

Laminæ compressed by hammering

A much better way is to "draw down" the spill by hammering the end of the bar first on the anvil and then with a "monkey tool", finally smoothing away the irregularities and protuberances with a "rose mill", driven by a brace or by a portable electric drill. If you follow this second method the laminæ are now—by hammering—pressed tightly together in the shoulder and along the spill, giving relatively additional strength in the very place where extra strength is most needed. All this is, I am aware, a consideration for the smithy; but it will also serve to bring home to designers one instance of the importance of providing for a modelled effect when they are laying-out the scheme on paper.

In much the same connection you may often see wrought-iron objects which have been punched and chiselled on the surface. Surface decoration is a practice of which you should be careful: the subject really deserves a book to itself, being full of possibilities and of pitfalls. The standpoint from which you should approach the matter is simply: "Can the object do without it?" This is far more reasonable than to ask yourself: "Can the object carry it?" Punch marks and chisel cuts offer a ready outlet for the "decorator". They can be definitely right—or equally they can be quite wrong. They should be *simple* and *deep* in order to make it appear that the object has been lightly modelled. In point of fact there is not much difference between light modelling and heavy tooling.

Amongst the things which you will discover, when you can tear yourself away from that office stool to do a bit of hammering, is the fact that iron has a peculiar awareness and sensibility. It openly resists certain treatment, and is quick to tell you when it is being treated wrongly. It is one thing to torture the metal and it is quite another to cause it to flow gently and reasonably into a good-looking shape. Treated kindly it is a stuff which can be guided into many shapes in the hands of a crafty smith. When you handle it thus you can obtain surprising results. You can make it blossom like the bough, though you must be careful not to over-do this treatment; or you can make it merge quietly and usefully into many kinds of architectural environment. It is a grand experience to stand back and to regard that fine piece of ironwork which you

The abuse of the scroll

have made. There it is and in that shape it will stay for a long, long time, a tribute to the cunning and sympathy which you have bestowed on it.

Particularly happy in the design of wrought-iron work is the scroll, that lovely, vital motif which comes straight from Nature herself. It is the gentlest of all emblems, whereby it has been so much used in ironwork. But it is wasted and abortive unless it *flows*. There is a fashion among some designers and ironworkers to take the most unwarrantable liberties with the scroll: they seem to have forgotten, these people, the natural origin of the thing.

Scrolls rarely occur singly but more often in groups of twos or threes: it may be of interest, therefore, to consider the various ways of making

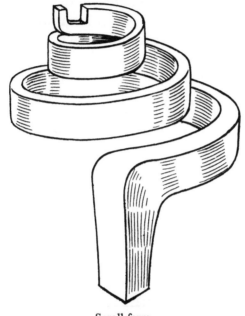

Scroll-form

them and the many ways in which you may join them together. It is generally supposed that the right way to "bend" a scroll is through the medium of a "scroll-form", this being a kind of mould resembling a scroll which has been pressed out from the centre so that it becomes a cone, with its apex formed by the centre. The practice is to fit your bit of iron into this apex and then to wind it down and around the "scroll-form", ultimately flattening it so that it lies in one plane only.

In my opinion this is not a right use of iron. It smells too much of the method of the mass producer. Once you have your scroll-form in the correct shape you can go on turning scrolls until sundown, all of them being exactly alike. At "The Devon Smithy" we do not use this device; we bend all our scrolls by sight, resting the iron on the beak of the anvil and tapping it into the proper shape with a hammer, bit by bit. This is a tricky business and not every ironworker can make scrolls in this way. But it produces excellent results, with the great advantage that each scroll is separately made and is therefore quite unique in its own way.

A scroll may finish at the centre in the form of a leaf or knob or simply by a gradual diminution of section; and there are some other ways, twin scrolls, expanded scrolls, etc., of which I will not trouble you with a description. There are one or two different ways in which you may join the scrolls. You can taper the adjoining scrolls and rivet them together. And after that you can proceed if you are so minded to put a collar round the riveted part. But at "The Devon Smithy" we always *weld* our scroll-work; and this is much the best way to do it, in contrast with some of the cheap, foreign ironwork which has found its way into this country in the past, in which light and flimsy scrolls are joined lightly and flimsily together by means of rivets and clips. Into these the moisture penetrates with most distressful results. In a later part of this book I shall tell you how to set about the process of welding and, if you follow carefully what I shall tell you, you will find after a time that it is much the best way in which to join scrolls together.

It is enough here to say that welding makes a homogeneous joint into which the moisture cannot penetrate, so that the scrolls will be safe and strong for a very long time.

Much of the rightness of decorative iron depends on the relative thicknesses of the bars which constitute the piece. For example, a length of railing is rather a dull affair when all its bars are of equal section. It is reasonable that the more important bars should be heavy, and the less important ones light. But it is a fact that you can discover an enormous number of examples in which attention has obviously not been given to this point. Squareness of bar seems to suit wrought iron very well. Round bars are rather smug and unsatisfactory. Perhaps this is due to the undecided "light and shade" which lie on their surface. Flat bars I would like to eliminate altogether save for the making of scroll-work. In a structural sense they are beastly things. They certainly look common, as if they had come out of an ironmonger's rather than out of a smith's shop. Flat bars are used by many smithies for the horizontal members of gates, grilles and railings where vertical bars pass through them.

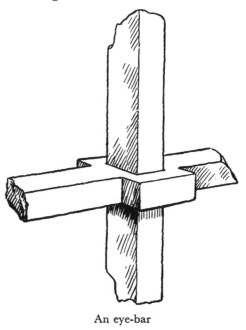

An eye-bar

A long time ago when my smithy had been under way at West Hill for a year or so I came to the conclusion that square iron was the ideal "section" in the building-up of decorative wrought iron. And this being so, it became rather a problem how to carry square verticals through square horizontal members. We got over the difficulty—after a little thought and a few experiments—by using square iron with *forged eyes* lying at proper intervals along the length of the bar. We have stuck to this method ever since.

Wrought iron is a resourceful metal when it finds its way into the hands of a crafty smith. It can be persuaded into an enormous number of shapes: then why on earth must some designers introduce *cast iron* into the scheme? I suppose that cast iron has a decorative value, though I find it hard to believe this. I hate it and so does every other decent smith: it is so obvious that this is the stuff whereof mass-production "articles" are made.

Now you can't turn out wrought-iron work in this way: it can't be made from a mould. Nor will it ever be made thus until we turn into a race of robots. No matter what the object may be, if it is of wrought iron it has been worked into shape by a man's strong hands and is a single, individual piece.

There is a fashion nowadays to make wrought-iron work look as though it had been beaten down by hand. In the old days the smith had to beat out his iron into straight bars just as into any other shape. There were no rolling mills round the corner, as there are nowadays, turning out beautiful straight bars of varying sections, all to suit his particular need. The iron arrived at the smithy in the form of a bloom—a kind of exaggerated doughnut in appearance—and from this the old smith forged the shapes and sizes which he happened to need.

It has often been maintained that in this arduous beating out from the lump lies the explanation of the rare occurrence of straight bars in examples of a date prior to the fourteenth century.

Getting back to the subject of making the bars look as though they had been beaten down by hand, this is seen to be legitimate and excellent when it occurs logically and inevitably as a result of work performed on them. The ancient smith's handiwork, a mass of jolly inexactitudes, is mighty good to look upon. Nowadays we get our material from the mills with much of the labour already done for us. The iron is in the form of long bars of 14–16 ft. and of varying sections; they are obviously the product of a machine.

Now it is a well-known fact, about which the more decent of us are heartily ashamed, that we make rubber to imitate tiles and carved wood to look like plaster; but let us draw the line when it comes to pretending that machine-rolled bars have been drawn down by hand. Nobody in his senses would imagine that they were other than machine-made. But in their ardent pursuit of the "hand-made" some anxious folk go bashing and brutalising these bars with a blow here and a blow there until the poor iron looks as though some metallivorous mouse had attacked it. Who ever heard of a carpet dealer letting moths into a carpet in order to give a genuine, ancient look about it? It is a deceit and a fake and no

PLATE IV

GRILLE FOR H.M. KING EDWARD VIII

Made at the Devon Smithy in 1931

designer worth his profession will specify it in any job which is being done for him.

These are some of the considerations which I like to keep in mind at "The Devon Smithy". It is very hard to do so; often enough I have tried to apply them to some job-of-work which we have been about to undertake; and I have realised the difficulty of the task. And on more occasions than I can remember I have looked at the finished piece and have wondered at the way in which it falls short of these principles.

Occasionally, rarely, I have succeeded in applying them fully: and on such occasions I have been convinced that they do not represent an ideal only, with all the impracticability which seems to characterise ideals. They are more than this; they represent the first principles of designing in wrought iron. I repeat the advice which I have already given you: go down to the smithy and beat iron, and you will find out for yourself that I have told you the truth.

CHAPTER VI

STRAIGHTWAY HEAD

1929 brought a great increase in work, and it was in this year that I first did work for Rosita Forbes. I made for her a masterful fine pair of gryphons, which were carved in wood and overlaid with sheet iron. Those gryphons took a shocking long time to

One of the gryphons

make. We sweated and shed tears of worry and vexation before we got them finished. I will tell you how we set to work on each of them.

First of all we found a good, straight, knot-free piece of pine which we carved into shape with chisels in the usual way. Then we took a piece of

18-gauge sheet iron, cut it up into small pieces and shaped and moulded each one of these pieces over a small part of the surface of the bird, following the undulations so that the pieces should fit precisely.

Starting on the head we would shape out one of the eyelids, doming the metal into a depression in a wood block and then tacking it in position with copper nails. Then we would trim the edges to the best advantage so that they should be a perfect fit with the pieces which were to lie adjacently; these in turn we would model and dome and shape and fasten into position with copper nails. This in itself was an immense labour and when all these small pieces were made the adjacent edges had to be soldered together.

You must be very careful in work like this, for unless each piece fits snugly into its next-door neighbour you will be tempted to use force to spring it down when you are laying on your solder. And though the solder may appear to be holding the edges firmly and without strain their tendency is to fly apart; which one day they will succeed in doing so that the damp will get into the wood with horrid results.

There were over one hundred and fifty moulded pieces in each of those two gryphons and we weren't sorry to complete them. When they were finished Rosita Forbes discovered that they weren't what

4-2

she wanted. We took them back and mounted them on tree stumps outside my office, overlooking the road; people in cars used to stop and stare and

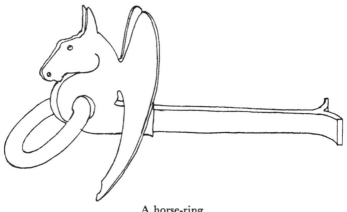

A horse-ring

sometimes to come in and ask me of what "period" they might be.

George, my foreman, always used to say that one of them—the hen bird, he was certain—attacked him one night. But as George was never able to tell me which was the cock and which the hen I didn't take him seriously.

I sold them eventually to Mrs Hart of Feniton.

In September we made a horse-ring for Lady Wedgwood. In terms of appropriateness of design, I think that this horse-ring is one of the best things ever produced at my smithy. It is made with the hammer only, and beaten into shape in the way which iron seems to like. Neither cutting nor filing have any part in its making. The only mechanical process involved is the use of the drilling machine to make the hole where the ring passes through the body.

Shoeing at West Hill had now died a natural and painless death so far as I was concerned. It had involved hard work and small pay and no great volume of thanks for the trouble which we had taken. So the farmers were left to look after themselves and went elsewhere. Very occasionally we would tighten up a shoe and then I would look back, reminiscently and gratefully and humbly, to those days when we used to depend on it; and I would reflect that after all shoeing is a very good introduction to the craft of decorative wrought-iron working.

It began to grow on me that we were getting mighty cramped for room in my smithy at West Hill. I had only two fires, the original brick one and a portable forge which I had bought later, a poor thing on which it was only possible to take a small heat. It was clear that we must either expand the building or build a new smithy.

Jobs of work of one kind and another had taken me often enough into Exeter, up the rise to Prickly Pear, to the right at the cross-roads and then to the left at "Exmouth Cross", by White's farm: and so with Straightway Head woods on the right to the junction where this, the Ottery St Mary-Exeter road, forks into the London-Exeter highway. Whenever I went this way and reached the fork I would slow down and turn my head to look at the woods. What a site for a new smithy, I used to think; the oaks and firs and chestnut trees were a joy in themselves and you could stand in front of them, as I have done on many an occasion, and look away to far-distant Dartmoor beyond the cupped fields and little square-cut woods lying between.

Soon I got into the habit of stopping my car and climbing on to the bank to examine the place more closely; and whilst one half of me was lost in a vague, unexpressed wish for the place, the business man in me would begin to guess at the number of cars which might be expected to pass it on the London highway on a summer's afternoon; and what percentage of these held potential customers; and what proportion of these in turn would stop, investigate and buy from me, always supposing that I could contrive to build a smithy in this place.

A kind uncle, whom I'll never be able to thank enough, made it possible for me to start operations immediately.

I will not make a lengthy tale of how I bought the land from Major Imbert Terry and set on foot the operations which led to the building of a new smithy among the trees of Straightway Head. It was an exciting business. My friend Robertson—the architect—and I had many an earnest consultation regarding windows and doors and the best design for the hearths before this early stage was reached.

One of the jobs which we had to do in connection with the new smithy was to find water. To this end I engaged Mr Beavis, the Postmaster of Aylesbeare, and invited some of my friends to come and watch him working the ground to find the best point at which to sink the well. It is an uncanny business. Beavis does not use a stick, but walks along with his hands stretched out in front of him, looking like a figure in an Egyptian frieze. As he draws near to water his hands tremble and shake like the twigs of a tree in the breeze. Presently they wave up and down or dart to and fro in jerky spasms. Finally, as he comes to the spot where the water affects him the most strongly, the hidden power racks and twists him so that he staggers this way and that. An uncanny business; several of my men can do it and so can Robertson. It appears to be a fairly common accomplishment in this part of the country. But I can't do it.

Beavis found a spring in the very corner of my ground, and there we sunk a well and found water at 24 ft. It is a good well. During the dry summer of 1930 it held an abundance of water.

In May, 1929, the smithy was springing up. The omens must have been favourable, for one of the labourers discovered a half-guinea piece of George II a foot under the surface. I'll make a bet that this coin was part of the loot from some little piece of highway robbery, for the site must have been ideal for this sort of enterprise in days gone by.

In September we moved into the new smithy at Straightway Head.

It was an enormous improvement on the first forge at West Hill. It was lighter and better ventilated, with long deep benches and a brick floor for the men to stand on when working at anvil or vice. There were four fires in the shape of a pair of double hearths. There was ample room inside the smithy for any job likely to come our way.

I paid great heed to the importance of having good lighting, as you can't do fine work in the gloom. I brought water from the well to basins and fitted the forges with water-cooled tue irons on the principle of the domestic hot-water system; this was a great improvement on the solid tue of the single hearth at West Hill. Also, I had a little office and show-room and a small, well-lighted drawing office at the top of a flight of steps. You see, I wasn't going to take any chances of being pinched for room.

We moved into the smithy; you can imagine my feelings—they were very mixed—at taking leave of the little forge at West Hill. This was the place where I had sweated and learned and taught myself the rudiments of blacksmithing. Now I was leaving it for good. It was sold to a villager across the road, who later transformed it into a couple of unromantic cottages.

The "move" from the old smithy to the new was accomplished in one day and with the loss of only one day's work. All the gear—the blowers, anvils, tools and such—was taken up the hill in lorries. The new smithy had been wired and a concrete bed built in the engine room; the Kohler plant was unshipped, transferred and fitted up so that we were provided with electric power with less than two days' delay.

I must tell you something about my men, George Davey, Ted Scott, Harry Potter and the rest of them.

When I bought the West Hill forge from Harry Potter, in June, 1926, he stayed on to work for me. He and I were the only two in the smithy until October of that year.

The work consisted mainly of shoeing and the repair of various implements: in this line of business there wasn't much that Harry didn't know, he being mighty crafty with his fingers and artful of purpose when it came to making up his mind to overcome a technical difficulty. But later on when I began to establish a "connection" for decorative wrought iron it became clear that I could increase my production, which would necessitate my finding another man to help with the work.

In October I put an advertisement in a local paper and received a shoal of replies. One of them was

from a George Davey: it sounded promising. It was
posted from an address in Wellington. So I went
over there to interview the writer and to see what
sort of a fellow he was. I took with me a bit of
ironwork for him to copy, by way of a practical trial
of what he could do. The upshot of the whole business was that I engaged him. In this way George
Davey came to "The Devon Smithy" and has been
with me ever since.[1]

To look at George you'd never think that he'd
"got it in him". He is small; and though you can
see at a glance that he is wiry and strong and without
an ounce of superfluous flesh on his bones, yet you'd
be amazed at the enormous energy which he can
muster and at the way in which he handles heavy iron.

Apart from his own energy George has the very
useful knack of infecting the other lads with his own
boyish enthusiasm. When they are all at work the
job fairly flies through their fingers. Besides this he
has the most charming manner and way of address:
the number of innocent, unsuspecting persons who
come visiting to my smithy, arriving with the
avowed object of "looking round" but leaving with
one of the firm's products tucked under an arm, is
legion. George has a very taking way with him, as
most of my visitors remark. When I go away for
a few days I go with a care-free mind, for I know
that the work proceeds, and rather more actively

[1] Written in 1932.

than when I am nearby. I never doubt that whenever I may choose to return I shall find them hard at it and as busy as bees.

Whilst helping me to run the West Hill forge Harry Potter was the owner of a little bicycle and gramophone-record shop adjoining the Post Office. Early in 1927 he had to leave me for a time in order to give more attention to this; for a time I was short-handed.

Ted Scott came to me in July of that year and has been with me ever since. He is a likeable chap and has done some good work for me, being at his best at the making of medium-sized, "crafty" pieces of ironwork.

In September, 1929, Harry Potter came to me again for a while to help us with the work; but nowadays he has gone back to West Hill where he looks after his bicycle business, sells petrol and motor oils, and occasionally makes a few pokers, tongs and trivets for me when we are especially hard pressed at my smithy.

The first apprentice whom we engaged was unluckily rather small. This in itself might have been no disadvantage only that he combined with it a cheekiness the like of which, George said, had never been heard in any smith's shop of his experience. This fine fellow came to us in December, 1926, and left us—or did we leave him?—on January 7th, 1927.

Thereafter we had a succession of boys to help us. Some of them were promising, but their parents took them away just when they had learned a bit and were getting useful; some were useful but cheeky, and it was hard to decide which quality was more noticeable. Others again were useless *and* cheeky, duds of the most hopeless kind—idle, wasteful, irresponsible.

One of the first things I noticed on getting into the new smithy was the strange and variegated flow of persons and things which goes by on the main road. All sorts of queer people seem to have business towards Exeter or Honiton. Gypsies and missionaries and circuses on tour come slowly up the hill towards London or put on their brakes as they reach my place, if they are going the other way, towards Exeter.

In the summer of 1930 we were invaded by flocks of visitors to my smithy. Visitors always choose a particular kind of day on which to come here— a day of bright sky with fleecy clouds and a strong breeze and with the temperature rather low; the kind of weather which often comes in September. No matter what the time of year, when a day of this kind comes along I know quite certainly that I shall have visitors at "The Devon Smithy".

But we have visitors and visitors! Some of them are civil and some of them are not. Some of them arrive in a very overheated state, and leaning negligently on the bottom half of my office door breathe the hopeful words, "A pint of bitter please." It breaks my heart to disillusion them.

I was once invaded by two large and perspiring ladies who were cruising the West Country in an Austin "Seven". They marched into my office, dropped into my easy chairs and demanded a "port and lemon" apiece. I was so sorry for them that I offered them a drink of cider of which I used to keep a little store; only to be asked angrily what I meant by it, young man?

Apart from its business interest the work of the smithy has always enthralled me and will always do so. Nowadays I do not have much opportunity to get into the forge, as office work and designing keep me from it. I wish it were otherwise: there is a primitive feeling about the place, when the forges are blazing and the anvils are singing away like church bells. I get what Americans call "a kick out of it" every time I clap my eyes on the place on my way here of a morning.

It is such great good fun to be your own master, isn't it? Far better than sitting on a stool in another man's office in return for a weekly wage or a monthly salary, paid to you in exchange for a contribution of your time and energy rather than for some complete production on your part. I'd rather scratch the ground as my own master than be absorbed in any capacity into a big organisation in which any identity which I might have would be lost. Here at my smithy I am always designing and making something new for some new acquaintance, and handling a little money as the result of the transaction. Aren't these enough to keep anyone happy at his job? I know that I am happy.

Considering all these things I recollect with gratitude those early places and people, farmers and villagers and gypsies and kind friends who helped to bring "The Devon Smithy" into being. I remember the time when we depended on shoeing and on the repair of farm implements. You will understand my believing that these are experiences to be thankful for, as they are a sound introduction to the design and practice of this craft.

CHAPTER VII

IRON

Apart from the scientific interest of the subject, it is useful to know something of the way in which bar iron, the raw material of the wrought-iron worker, is manufactured.

From practical experience I know that there are many good reasons why the wrought-iron worker should use only the very best brand on which he can lay his hands. In the first place, iron is a negligible factor in the cost of production. The difference in the cost of the iron content of a gate selling for £50 and of another gate selling for £500 will be a matter of a sovereign or two only. This is only another way of saying that the expensive item in the cost of production is the labour. This being the case, why use any but the best iron?

Besides this the whole purpose of ironwork is, as I have shown, to secure or defend persons or places. Much of the detail of a large wrought-iron grille may be intricate to a degree; you may spend hundreds of pounds worth of labour in forging and fixing the various components, only to find yourself compelled by the fracture of a key-part of the grille to take the whole thing to pieces again and then to rebuild it. All this could have been avoided if you had used good iron.

There is much low-grade material on the market nowadays; a huge production of mild steel, which is put out at a comparatively low price, has led to a certain confusion and some ironworkers seem to find it a great temptation to use mild steel in place of genuine wrought iron.

By far the most important objection to the use of mild steel is that this metal is cold-hearted stuff, unsympathetic, flinty and possessing none of the easy-going qualities of wrought iron. This may strike you as being a fantastic distinction; but if you go into a smithy and pick up two bits of metal—one of wrought iron and the other of mild steel—and bring each one to a "welding heat" so that you can model it with a hammer, you will quickly discover that I have told you the truth. To define the difference more closely (yet non-technically) is very difficult. Mild steel seems to be less of a "grainy" metal than wrought iron; its laminæ are less pronounced; yet it is lacking in that plastic quality which makes wrought iron so easy to handle, when you know how to do this.

It is safe to say that for the purposes of decorative ironwork any wrought iron is better than the best brand of mild steel which the ironworker can get; but it is still of the utmost importance that he should get a good brand and stick to it and that he should be quite certain that it is the kind of iron which it pretends to be.

The nature and the manufacture of the so-called "genuine puddled wrought iron" is dealt with more or less fully in a number of text-books. We may leave high technicalities to the expert, who enjoys such matters. But you ought to know just enough about the subject to be able to listen intelligently when you meet that expert and he becomes eloquent.

The process is an indirect one; from ore to pig iron, from pig iron to puddled bar and from puddled bar to finished malleable iron bar. It is not commercially practicable to produce finished malleable iron direct from the ore, though this can be done.

The iron ore or iron stone is smelted in a vertical furnace known as a blast furnace.

The furnace charge consists of fuel, ore and flux in suitable proportions. The object of the flux is to make readily fusible those mineral impurities in iron which—even in the intense heat of the blast furnace —would otherwise remain infusible. The exact nature of the flux varies in accordance with the nature of the ore used. But its object is always the same; it is calculated to help in the production of the greatest proportionate quantity of relatively pure iron. The usual fluxing material employed is limestone.

Among the devices for utilising to the fullest extent the heat generated by combustion in the furnace is the hot-air blast, which speeds up the process.

On being drawn from the furnace the molten

iron is run into channels formed in a bed of sand, and is there allowed to cool and solidify. This iron is known as pig iron, the size of the pigs being usually from 3 ft. to 4 ft. long and weighing from 1 cwt. to 2 cwt. each. Pig iron is really the raw material of the malleable iron manufacturer, and it is in his works that it is subjected to the operation known as puddling.

The object of puddling is to eliminate as far as may be possible the impurities—such as carbon, silicon, sulphur and phosphorus—present in the pig iron. Each of these impurities has a definite and recognised effect on the iron. For example, if there is too much phosphorus or silicon present the iron becomes what is known as "cold-short", *i.e.* brittle when cold. On the other hand, an excess of sulphur produces a different effect, the iron becoming "hot-short", *i.e.* brittle when hot.

The puddling furnace which is the scene of the next process consists of two parts: one of these is called the grate, the other being the hearth.

The two chambers are separated by a partition, the purpose of which is to allow the flames from the grate to play upon the pig iron on the hearth without allowing the iron to come into contact with the fuel.

The preparation of the puddling furnace before it can be used involves a ritual of its own. The puddler has to line the hearth of his furnace with a "fettling" material consisting of tap cinder. So that the lining of tap cinder may have the necessary smooth surface it is covered with a paste made from "purple ore".

The cast-iron bottom plate of the hearth is protected by a layer of what is known as "hammer slag" or "mill scale". After the furnace has been lit it takes four to five hours to melt the slag, after which the furnace is allowed to cool so that the fluid cinder obtained may set hard upon the plates. The furnace is now ready for puddling, and the charge of pig iron is put inside.

When the furnace is fully charged the door is shut and all crevices and cracks carefully stopped up so that no air may enter. A supply of coal is put into the grate for the purpose of melting the charge. In about twelve minutes the top part of the pig iron becomes red hot, when the underhand puddler turns it over to expose the cooler parts of the metal to the heat. His object in doing this is to arrange for the whole bulk of pig iron to melt as nearly as possible at one and the same time.

Within half an hour from the time of charging the puddling furnace the iron lies on the hearth in a liquid state, covered with melted slag. The underhand puddler now takes hold of a special tool called a "rabble" and stirs the material as it lies on the hearth. The result of this stirring is that the carbon in the metal combines with the oxygen of the slag. Carbonic gas is given off and the iron expands.

At this stage the charge is said to "boil". As the puddler vigorously works and stirs the charge the iron arrives at a stage which is known as "coming to nature", and takes the form of a sponge-like mass. The puddler collects this mass and forms it into rough balls.

As each ball is withdrawn from the furnace it is taken by the underhand puddler to a steam-hammer and vigorously hammered into a bloom.

This hammering is known as "shingling", and has the effect of expelling cinder from the ball. After being hammered the blooms are taken to the forge mill and are there rolled down into flat, heavy bars, known as puddled bars.

The process is now nearly complete. These puddled bars, when cool, are cut into suitable lengths and formed into piles, which are brought to a welding heat in reheating furnaces and are then taken direct to the bar mill, where they are rolled into a multitude of different shapes and sizes.

This is the briefest description of a long and complicated process, it being impossible in a work of this kind to do justice to the subject. It is necessarily incomplete, but it will I hope give the lay reader some notion of the manner whereby the crude ore arrives at the state in which it is serviceable to the decorative wrought-iron worker.

CHAPTER VIII

THE TOOLS OF THE SMITH

Before you can properly begin to design decorative wrought-iron work you must, as I have several times told you, get acquainted with the technique of the smith. And it is clear that your first lesson—as it will be the first lesson of any apprentice to any craft —will be to learn the names of the various tools and the manner in which each of them is used.

There are certain tools which are common to all smithies—such as the HEARTH and BELLOWS, WATER-TROUGH, ANVIL and ANVIL-BLOCK, HAMMERS and TONGS, SLEDGE-HAMMERS, plain TOP- and BOTTOM-TOOLS, PUNCHES and the like. The needs of the worker in decorative wrought iron have added to this simple equipment: the craft has grown in complication and cunning with the result that these simple tools are not enough for him, every job tending to develop its own specific tool, jig, template or other contrivance. Later on I shall tell you how to set about the making of a candlestick. This needs a special rim tool. Scroll-work which figures so happily in many a wrought-iron work design needs a little tool known as a "dog" when you come finally to adjust it. You can very easily see that the tendency is towards such elaboration of equipment that there will be many tools and

appliances in his shop for which the crafty smith has
no specific name. They came into being to deal with
some tricky problem and now their work is done.
Until such time as another job of that particular
kind comes along they will lie in a corner of the
forge, nameless and only dimly recollected. It is
therefore difficult to make a complete list, a catalogue
of all the tools of the smith, for their name is legion.
At "The Devon Smithy" my own inclination lies
towards simplifying rather than towards elaborating
the equipment of my forges. I will go farther and
say that the equipment of a country forge is all that
is necessary for the designing and making of decorative ironwork of a high order.

This is a machine age and the majority of us are
quick to suppose that the responsibility for making
anything can be entrusted to a piece of machinery.
But the disadvantage of the machine is that it com-
pletely stereotypes everything which it handles.

When all is taken into account it is the combination
of steady hand and crafty eye which has produced
and ever will produce the most eyeable and enduring
examples; no amount of button pushing and lever
pulling will compensate the absence of that inde-
finable yet magical thing which is known as Individuality. The more tools you add to the equipment
of your smithy, the more surely will you obliterate
individuality. If your object, like mine, is the production of a few decent examples of good design

and good workmanship without distressing yourself too greatly concerning "rate of production",—that watchword of the mass producer—then the simple tools will suffice and you will be the happier in being in a position to guide them and to escape the ignominy of being guided by them. I know little of mass-production methods; but I discovered a long time ago that there were two ways of making a dozen four-legged trivets. One way consisted in forging forty-eight legs and joining them to twelve frames. That was a kind of mass production, I suppose; it brought the most rotten results. The alternative way was to make each trivet separately; first hammering out four legs, then the frame, all in the way which I shall describe to you presently, which answers very well indeed. For each trivet made in this way differs a little from its neighbour: each one shows a measure of the personal touch and thereby possesses individuality. But industry is so hypnotised by democratic expediency that it clings to the other method: a fact which explains why a great many people—myself included—are unable to believe that the New Jerusalem about which we hear so much will be much different from one of our big industrial towns.

In the meantime I am consoled by the fact that I am able, on picking up a piece of finished ironwork which has been made at my smithy, to know which of my men has made it. It has his signature in various places, readily discernible to me. This is one of the smaller pleasures which I get out of blacksmithing.

The ideal way to run a smithy is to operate it by hand-power throughout, in blowing the bellows, drilling, hacksawing and the like. It is a fact that even a little operation such as the drilling of a rivet hole seems to impart an extra dignity to the iron when it is performed by hand-power.

The HEARTHS which I built at Straightway Head are of brick—6 ft. wide, 4 ft. deep and 3 ft. 6 in. high. They contain two TUES apiece so that each hearth may carry two fires, which are most useful when we want to heat two heavy pieces of iron for welding.

Over the hearth is a COWL, which carries away the smoke and fumes *via* the CHIMNEY-STACK into the open air. It is a matter of great importance that your chimneys should "draw" well in the prevailing wind at least, else your smiths will have the choking fumes in their faces while they are at work.

For myself I have a liking for BELLOWS in preference to mechanical blowers of any kind. This is not a matter of sentiment only, for there is no doubt that with bellows you can regulate the heat of your fire to better advantage than you can with the more mechanical but less sensitive fan-blower. When I built my present smithy I fitted it, true enough, with blowers; but this was on account of my having to save every inch of space, the old-fashioned bellows taking up rather a lot of room. I rather regretted this at the time as the "up-and-down" kind are much more genuine besides being amusing.

The main hearth of my forge at West Hill had these old-fashioned bellows. They were packed away in a little room behind the hearth and chimney-stack; you had to worm yourself through a low archway in the dividing wall if you wanted to get at them for any purpose. They were never perfectly

Pear-shaped bellows

airtight, those bellows: they would squeak and whistle and make queer, clanking noises where the seams were loose or the working-mechanism worn. But they struck just the right pagan note which every country smithy should have. Once a year an ancient woman carrying a carpet bag would appear in the smithy doorway and announce that she had come to mend the "Bellowses". Then armed with a candle-end she would creep behind the hearth

and there would be subterranean sounds, tappings
and scratchings and a swear-word or two until
sundown when the job would be done in time for
the smithy to be locked up for the night. She would
reappear, dishevelled and more witch-like than ever
and ask 5s. for her trouble. It was well worth the
money, for she certainly knew how to do the job.
When we went into the dark cavern next day we
would find the holes neatly patched, the seam-
stitching tightened up and made secure and all
fast and strong, good for another twelve months'
work. So that when I built the new smithy in
Straightway Head woods I was sorry not to be able
to equip it with the old-fashioned kind of bellows.
The West Hill bellows I brought with me and fixed
outside my office; there you may see them as you
dash past on the main road. They look rather
melancholy in their disuse.

Standing close in front of the hearth is the
TROUGH which is simply a receptacle for water,
fixed to the front of the hearth. It is useful when you
want to douse the iron or tongs, chisels and so on
so that they may be made cool enough to handle.

Accessory to the hearth are the SHOVELS, POKERS
and WATERING-CAN.

The watering-can is used for cooling hot iron in
some specific place; for example, if you want to
cool the whole piece of iron you can drop it into the
trough. But when you are making a twist in a long

bar you have to be very careful that the twist comes
out evenly. You wind-up the bar a little bit at a time,
cooling it in front and behind the section which you
wish to twist. This is where the watering-can comes
in useful.

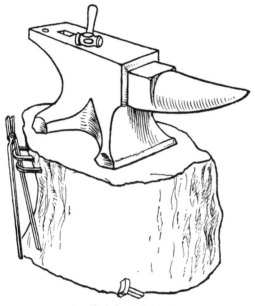

Anvil and anvil-block

Standing close beside the hearth and more or less
on a line with the water-trough are the ANVIL and
ANVIL-BLOCK. Anvils are of all shapes and sizes;
but the sort which we use are of the kind most
commonly met in country blacksmiths' shops—the
English anvil.

Each and every forging operation—that is to say, the process of altering the shape of the iron whilst it is hot—must be carried out on the top of the anvil, which should stand about 30 in. from the ground. This will be determined more or less by the height of the smith and what suits him best. On his left as he stands to work at it is the BEAK which is useful in bending scrolls and for drawing down small bars.

The ANVIL-BLOCK is a section of tree-trunk from good, seasoned timber. You sometimes see anvil-blocks made of metal. I don't like these myself: there is a springiness about a wood-supported anvil which makes it pleasant to use. Our best anvil has a clear, bell-like note when you strike it; so that you can hear the din of my smithy when you are half a mile away down the road.

TONGS. All the tongs which we use we make ourselves, and in this way we can be certain that they have good stuff in them. Beside this you need many kinds of tongs which you can't buy; so you have to set about making these for yourself. They are named according to the kind of jaws they have: WIDE or CLOSE, FLAT, ROUND, HALF-ROUND, SQUARE, THREE-SIDE, and so on.

When you want to alter iron of any section to a smaller sectional area you must forge it between TOP and BOTTOM SWAGES. The bottom swage fits into the top of the anvil in the swage-hole provided for it. The top swage is wrapped into a convenient wire handle or is held in a shaft. The "work" is

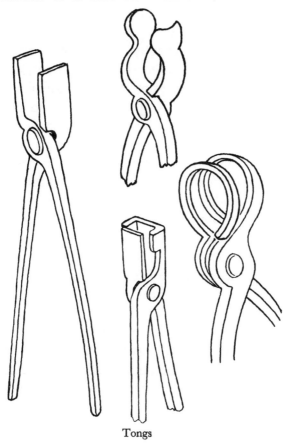

Tongs

placed between the two and the top swage is struck with the hammer, or with a SLEDGE—if it is very heavy work.

FULLERS are very useful when you want to make a depression or channel in a piece of iron. They are available as top-tools or as bottom-tools. But in working a bottom-fuller you have to be very careful to keep the work exactly on top of it and in its proper position. The secret in this operation lies in making a little depression on the underside of the work before turning it upside down—and you may do the same thing to the remaining surface before you start your fullering operation. This groove which you have made will be found helpful in preventing the work from slipping off the bottom-fuller. With an easy mind you can get Cyril the apprentice to strike a few blows for you with the sledge.

Additionally there are HOT and COLD SETS with which you cut the iron. They are held in a twist of wire (or they may be fitted with a hammer-shaft) and are struck atop with a sledge.

Used for the same purpose but in a different way are the CUTTERS which are fixed vertically in the CUTTER-HOLE of the anvil. Thus you can see that there is more than one method of cutting off a piece of iron on the anvil, apart from putting it in the SHEARS. You can cut it hot or cold: you can lay it on the flat of the anvil and use a hammer or a sledge-hammer to divide it with a hot set at the appropriate place. Or you can lay it on the sharp upper edge of the cutter and hit it a few blows on top. If you cut it cold you must use a cold set.

Apart from these there are HOT and COLD CHISELS —which are like the ordinary chisels you see in any fitting shop. They are used in cases where it would be awkward to lay the work on a cutter or to use a set.

Of all the PUNCHES (SQUARE, ROUND, SLOTTING, etc.), I cannot possibly speak. There are an enormous number of different kinds, each one of which has its particular use.

Most of these punches we make for ourselves; and herein lies much of the charm of this old craft of smithing—the sheer necessity of making your own tools, it being impossible to buy them elsewhere. As I have said in another part of this book the smith is the tool-maker for every other trade, craft and profession, and not least for himself.

Sometimes we have to make a few hundred hand-made nails; "five-clout nails", they are called. In making these you have to use a NAIL-TOOL which is a short bar of iron with a hole in one end of it.

In forging one of these nails you take a bit of small iron, draw it down to a point, gauge the right length and partially sever it on the cutter. Then you put the pointed end through the nail-tool and break it off, leaving the nail—complete but without its head —in the nail-tool. You lay the whole thing over the front edge of the anvil and put on five quick, heavy blows with your hammer at the place where the head is to be. You put one blow for each corner and one

for the top, giving the head five facets, just as you
would cut a diamond. And you have to do all this

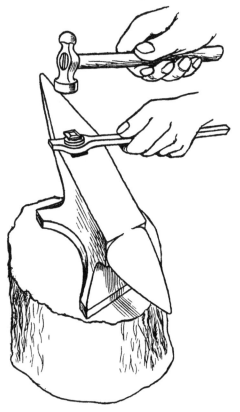

Using a nail-tool

during the very short space in which the iron is
cooling. You now know the meaning of the expression "Strike while the iron is hot", and why these
are called "five-clout nails".

SCROLLING-DOGS are convenient when you want to adjust the sweep of a scroll. You very often need to do this when you find that a piece of scroll-work will not quite fit into its appointed place.

The MEASURING ROD is a most convenient tool when you want to see whether a rectangular frame-work—such as the framework of a gate—is square between all pairs of sides. You might check this by gauging the *angles* at the corners with a square.

Scrolling-dog

This is a fairly accurate method as far as it goes. But unless your square is of the adjustable kind— which kind is easily damaged—it will only show a general, *angular* error which is hard to determine exactly. On the other hand if you compare the two *diagonals* you will be able to measure a discrepancy in *length* and will thus get a much better idea of how far the gate is from being absolutely square. This is where your measuring rod is useful.

The TYRING WHEEL is used for measuring distances circumferentially. Its original use by the smith comes when he wants to bond a new tyre on to a cart wheel. Being a crafty fellow he likes to know the exact amount of iron to cut off, allowing a reasonable extra for wastage. He measures round the rim of the wheel with the tyring wheel, noting the number of complete revolutions and "the bit left over", and then goes on to reproduce this length on the bar of iron which he has to cut. It is a simple device, utterly reliable and sensible and otherwise excellent.

Now I have no space to tell you much about the hundred and one other tools, fixed and portable. For the fact is that I have already described to you enough for you to be able to recognise and give a name to everything which you are likely to meet in the ordinary smith's shop.

Now, well acquainted with these, you may begin to consider the technique of their use.

CHAPTER IX

WELDING AND SCROLL-WORK

To tabulate all the tricks and devices and subtleties to which the crafty smith has recourse, at one time or another, would be wearisome. A piece of iron-work may be simple or complicated or between the two. The simplest ironwork is, practically speaking, that which is devoid of *construction*—which has been worked out of one piece, probably by the sole use of the hammer and perhaps with the aid of punches.

As I have indicated, it is in these simpler, more natural expressions that smith's work is at its best. For here the smith has an opportunity to treat the metal plastically: he is not called upon to cut and file and fit it, the latter processes belonging far more legitimately to the craft of the locksmith. In much the same way that a sculptor goes to work on his clay, so the understanding smith should go to work on his iron, doing all that he can with that chief tool of smithcraft, the hammer.

Merely to consider a complicated piece of iron-work, like a gate or a piece of railing, is to consider something which involves more than one process, which may be said to be a problem in *construction*, involving much *joining together*.

On the face of it the act of joining together separate pieces of iron is in itself contrary to the foregoing arguments concerning the nature of iron. Happily, however, the craft of the smith has come to the rescue with a primitive, adequate and thoroughly satisfactory method, which is known as WELDING.

Welding is the best way of joining one piece of iron to another. There are a great number of other methods which you are bound to employ when you build up a complicated piece of ironwork, but none of these comes up to this ancient process which I will describe to you.

Welding is the act of joining one piece of iron to another under heat and with the aid of the hammer, the heat having reduced the respective ends of the two pieces to a sparkling, plastic condition. I can do no better, I think, than to tell you how to set about the making of a lap-weld, which is the simplest and most frequently used of all the many kinds of welding.

Suppose that you want to weld two bits of $\frac{3}{4}$ in. square iron together; you first of all get a good, well-banked fire going strongly on the hearth. Then you take your iron, put the ends into the fire and get them white and UPSET them.

Upsetting is the name given to the act of thickening the metal at the end where it will be welded to the other piece. It is achieved quite simply by bumping or hammering the hot end horizontally against the inner face or vertically on the top of the anvil. This compresses the end and makes it thicker.

You must do this to both bits of iron, and then it will

be time to SCARF the ends. Scarfing is the process of making the end ready to meet and fit snugly to the end of the corresponding piece. You do it with the hammer or you might use a small fuller. The procedure has to include the drawing out of a lip. The two scarfed ends will now fit more or less closely together.

The iron is now cold; it must be put back into the fire and brought up to an even heat. Under your watchful scrutiny the surfaces of the two bits of iron will presently appear to take on a shimmering, fluid appearance. It is time to whip them from the fire and transfer them to the anvil. If you think that this condition is easy to recognise, you are mistaken. Until you know how to do it you may heat dozens of pairs and find it mighty difficult to bring the two bits to the same temperature simultaneously. You must watch very carefully, and with luck and increasing skill you will learn the trick of it.

You have seen the two pieces arrive at this state which I have described; you have whipped them out of the fire and have laid one of them on the anvil top, the other one being in its proper position so that the scarfed ends meet closely. Now you must hammer them together. And, whatever you do, go lightly at the beginning until the two are properly stuck together, gradually letting your blows fall more heavily as the iron cools. But don't let it get too cold! Now you will find to your surprise and pleasure that the two bits of iron are one with a slight bulge to show where they were united. You now perceive the full purpose of "upsetting" the ends of each piece before you welded them. If you hadn't done so there would have been a "waist" round about the bulge, which would have been caused by the hammer striking the iron on either side of the joint. As things are with your present welded joint, you can easily reduce the bulge by hammering, by rasping or by both; but preferably by hammering.

Of one thing you must be particularly careful— to avoid burning the iron by excessive heat. You can easily do this; and though it may be an inspiring thing to see those dazzling, golden sparks rise from the bed of the fire, it represents a great waste of good iron and possibly the spoiling of the piece.

The making of scroll-work is tricksome. Some people use complicated "scroll-forms" and "starters", "scroll-forks" and Heaven-knows-what-else in making scrolls. But if you've got a good eye you won't want any of these. Good iron, an anvil, a hammer, one or two pairs of "dogs" (which are illustrated in another part of this book[1]) and a stout heart will see you through any problem of this kind, however intricate; for they are all that you want for making many kinds of scroll-work. If you have a good eye and the cunning to make a scroll flow

[1] Scrolling-dog, p. 81.

gently and simply from its origin to its lawful destination, then the simplest tools will be all that you'll need. Need I add that a multitude of artifices and gadgets will not atone for your being ham-handed and boss-eyed. Scroll-work, intelligently wrought, is a fine way of expressing the character of wrought iron.

The first thing to do is to draw the scroll-work in full size on a flat sheet of iron. This is better than drawing it on a piece of paper, as continual comparison with hot iron will soon burn the flimsy sheet.

A scroll-panel

Lay out the scroll-work on the sheet iron and then paint it with black paint. You start with Section A. Pick up an appropriate length of $\frac{3}{4}$ in. × $\frac{1}{4}$ in. bar and thin it down at the end for about 5 in. Making use of the beak of the anvil, tap it round until you have brought it to the shape of the top scroll A (as far as X, where the scrolls meet). Do likewise with B up to the same point X. Now hold the scrolls together in a pair of medium-jawed tongs, taking care to see that they are in their proper respective places. Drill a small hole—say $\frac{3}{16}$ in.—through both at *X*, and bind them together with a $\frac{3}{16}$ in. rivet. Holding them firmly with the tongs, put them into the fire and bring them to a welding heat. It is impossible to describe in detail how you do the operation. If you really want to learn how it is done you had better go and watch the operation in some

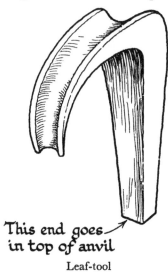

This end goes in top of anvil

Leaf-tool

smithy or other. Whip the lot out of the fire and, first lightly and then with heavier strokes as the iron cools, weld the sparkling mass into one homogeneous whole. There will of course be no need to look for the rivet, which will have been absorbed in the welding process. Your first two scrolls should now be identical with the full-size lay-out.

You must next forge out the leaf. You need a

special tool for this, as a "bottom-tool". Take a piece
of $\frac{3}{4}$ in. square iron about 12 in. long, heat it and
flatten out one end into a long thin leaf, an operation
which is quite easily done if you hit the iron in the
right place. Heat again and drive it down into the
special tool, whence it will emerge looking like the
leaf which you need, but without the crinkled edges.
It is an easy matter to get it hot again, to crinkle
these edges with a pair of taper round-nosed tongs
and to ginger it up to look like the original.

You must proceed in the way which I described,
to make and join and weld together the leaf with
the scroll C and the short intermediate length XY.
You can do these altogether, this being a better
way than welding the leaf to the intermediate and
then these two to the scroll C. Next you make scroll D
and weld it to the intermediate piece, YZ. Then
you make scroll E and weld it to D at Z. Finally,
you have only to judge the distance, upset and scarf
the respective ends at Y and weld them firmly
together, in order to produce a piece of scroll-work
similar to the drawing. But, oh! you will make
many attempts before you get it right, withal it
sounds so easy; for it isn't a bit easy in reality. The
art of welding is itself a fine one and so is the art
of estimating your distances. When welding scrolls
together a little prayer for understanding and a deal
of patience, good iron, a clear fire and a stout
heart—between these you ought to be successful.

CHAPTER X

MAKING A TRIVET

I will describe the way in which we make a certain
kind of trivet at my smithy. The trivet which you
are going to make looks like this.

You will see that it has a leg at each corner of a
rectangular frame. Now there are many ways in

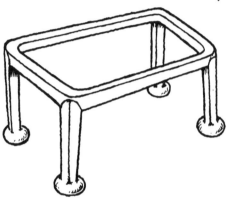

A trivet

which you may attach these legs to the frame: you
can make a spill on the end of each and provide for
it to pass through a drill-hole in its own corner of
the frame; after which you must "snap-over" the
bit which sticks out through the top of the hole. This
will look fairly well but not very well.

A better way of doing it would be to spread out
the top of the leg and to provide it with two small

drill-holes by which it could be riveted to the frame. This, if you did it neatly, would make quite a good job of it. But the best way of all would be to *weld* the leg to the corner of the frame, and that is the way in which we do it at my smithy.

First of all you must cut off a little piece of good, close-grained wrought iron of small square section ($\frac{3}{16}$ in. by $\frac{3}{16}$ in.) and 18 in. long. This you will use for the frame; and I chose this particular length so that the frame may be composed of two sides of 6 in. each and two sides of 3 in. each. Take up your ruler and measure to a point 3 in. from one end of the rod and there make a centre-punch mark. Travel another 3 in. and make a second centre-punch mark; then another 6 in. and finally another 3 in., in all cases leaving a centre-punch mark at these points. Your bar now looks like this:

Setting out the frame

Now you must make the legs of the trivet. The illustration shows that these legs have little knobs on their ends; you make the knobs in this way.

Stick a piece of $\frac{3}{16}$ in. by $\frac{3}{16}$ in. iron, 12 in. long, into the fire and get the apprentice to blow gently but steadily. When the tip is between red and white heats, but at considerably less than welding heat, whip it out of the fire, shake off the slag with a flick of your wrist and set it vertically on the anvil with the hot end downwards. "Upset" it in this position in the way that I have described elsewhere. You will now have a little lump on the end of the iron. Repeat this operation once or twice and you will have quite a fair-sized lump. Whatever you do be careful not to hit the iron when it has become cold or you'll ruin the whole thing. If you ignore this warning you will find that presently the metal will crack and split apart with horrid and sorrowful results; so that you could die for shame, and will in any case need to bring the lump to a welding heat if you want to repair the cracks. We will suppose, however, that you have learned how to do this properly. Put the iron into the fire and get it hot once more. Draw it out at a little below white heat, throw off the scale and begin to shape the lump into the rough semblance of a knob. In doing this you will find it convenient to make use of the front edge of the anvil, at the same time twisting the iron in order to benefit every side of it. After reheating you may with discernment and a measure of common sense succeed in producing a knob like this.

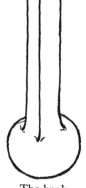

The knob

You deal with the pieces for the three other legs

in this way. And now that they are beautifully knobbed you must cut them off to their proper lengths—3 in. and a bit extra—and prepare them for welding to the frame.

You know that before you can weld one bit of iron to another you must first prepare the ends by what is known as "upsetting and scarfing", a process which I have described to you. So you may now do this to the ends of the legs.

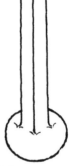

Now upset and scarf the frame at the points where you made the centre-punch marks. The upsetting is easy enough but you need a trick or two to scarf the bar

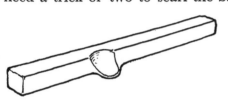

A leg and part of the frame upset and scarfed

at these marked points; you will find it convenient to carry out this operation on a corner of the anvil, laying the bar on the corner and striking it on top, which produces exactly the result which you need.

You may now proceed to weld the legs, one by one, to the frame. Put the scarfed end of a leg into the fire, together with a corresponding scarf on the frame. Bring them together to a sparkling heat and whip them out of the fire and on to the anvil; and with a gentle stroke of your hammer—half smiting and half pressing—lightly at first and heavily as you

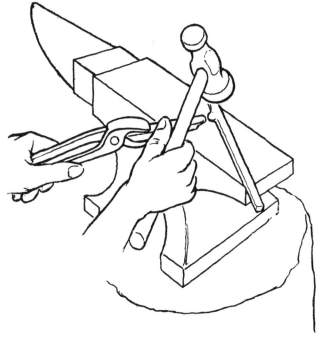

Welding a leg to the frame

go on, weld the two together. It sounds easy; and so it is when you know how to do it. The main difficulty lies in knowing just how to bring the two pieces simultaneously to the right temperature without burning either one or the other or both of them.

You perform this operation with each of the legs in turn. It remains only for you to bend the frame into shape; this needs a little care, as the corners occur just where the legs were welded. You must bring each joint to a white heat and make a kink in it. You can help matters by laying the outside of the corner in a bottom swage, at the same time striking a blow on the inside with a blunt-nosed fuller. You

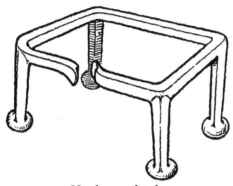

Nearly completed

will find that this produces just the kind of corner which you need.

The sides now occupy their right positions; you can adjust one or other in order to make the frame square. All that you now need to do is to upset and scarf the two ends of the frame, to weld them together and "draw" the weld so that the side is exactly 6 in. A touch with a file to remove those sharp edges— which would cut your fingers, etc.—a brush-full of paint and the job is done; so that your trivet now looks like the illustration at the beginning of this chapter.

But I assure you that I haven't told you a half of all the mysterious technique necessary for making even so simple a thing as a trivet. Such ritual as giving the anvil a passing tap between blows by the way of scaring off any evil that may be about the forge—and many other small conceits of this kind—the full significance of these may only be learned when you take off your coat, waistcoat and collar, and set about being a crafty smith yourself.

CHAPTER XI

MAKING A CANDLESTICK

The making of a candlestick is not a very considerable undertaking. When you compare it with some of the work which you are asked to carry out in the smithy you can see that it calls for little effort, imaginative or physical. The building of a gate, which may be so intricate as to keep you and your lads busy for three or four months and so cumbersome as to need several pairs of hands to move it or to manipulate it, this calls for a co-ordination of all the energy and dexterity and wise cunning which your men possess. The kind of craftiness which finds expression through the finger tips does not represent the whole function of the smith's shop. But it is very often needed when you have small pieces to make. Candlesticks are jolly things to make, with an old-fashioned feeling about them which is pleasant in these highly electrical days.

At "The Devon Smithy" we have from time to time made many candlesticks of one design or another. I will tell you how you should set about making one of these candlesticks so that you may be encouraged to make overtures to your village blacksmith with a view to borrowing his forge for this purpose.

You want a kind of craftiness different from the

craftiness which you needed in making that trivet about which I have just told you. The trivet was an exercise in smithing. The preparation of the legs and frame and the manner of fixing them together

A candlestick

in their rightful places, these constituted more or less of a technical problem; they were a problem in construction.

The candlestick on the other hand is going to exercise your wit in something beyond its mere making; for you need only to give it a glance to see that its principal feature is the curvature of the body between the candleholder and the base and the manner in which the handle and the base sweep into it. Therein lies the gist of the story which the candlestick tells to you and other discerning beholders.

The assumption is that you have been given—in the same way that one of my men would be given it if he had to do the job—a rough sketch of the candlestick. This you should be able to translate into the metal; and the way in which you set about doing it is this:

First of all sketch out your candlestick in full-size scale on a flat sheet of iron. Your purpose in doing this is so that you may have a drawing which will not be damaged by the iron; for you will constantly be comparing it with the hot metal. At my smithy we always transfer detail drawings on to sheet iron, sometimes through the medium of paint (if the piece is complicated) but more often by means of white chalk.

Now a little experiment with your lump of chalk will convince you that there are dozens of ways of drawing that sweep between the candleholder and the base, none of which seem however to be quite acceptable to your critical eye. You pick up the chalk and make a fresh start; and by some mysterious agency, by luck or by the help of the lame one, your hand gains a marvellous steadiness and your eye a sudden penetration; so that the curve which you have been pursuing materialises before you with results at once happy and encouraging.

In laying out your design you must be very careful to see that every part bulks rightly and harmoniously with its neighbour. For example, by making the flange and socket a little too big you will find that the whole candlestick looks overweighted. This how-ever is a matter which may not be apparent until after the candlestick is made, as it is difficult to obtain

Turning up the toes (i)

a real representation of the thing in terms of pencil and paper or to do justice to the metal; which is one of the many good reasons why ironworking should not be troubled with too much designing.

In this case you will know instinctively and beyond possibility of doubt when the design of your candle-stick has matured; so that you may begin to pick out your iron and set to work to carry the design into effect.

Take a piece of $\frac{5}{8}$ in. $\times$ $\frac{1}{4}$ in. bar, about 14 in. long, and get one end hot over a length of $3\frac{1}{2}$ in. to

4 in. With the hot set split this end along a length of $3\frac{1}{2}$ in. In doing this you must take care to divide the iron evenly along its centre line so that the two pieces will be of equal size and strength. Get the iron hot again and with a small hammer and the help of the anvil-beak spread these two ends apart.

The action of spreading these apart with the hammer will, if you are crafty about it, smooth away much of the roughness caused by your previous operation with the hot set. Get the iron hot again and square the tips of the two ends by laying them

Turning up the toes (ii)

on the cutter and striking off the roughness. You may now begin to curl the ends into the shape shown in your full-size lay-out.

You can do this partly by hammering the iron over the beak of the anvil and partly with the help of a pair of round-nosed pliers. When you have done this you must measure off the correct lengths from the union of these scrolls to the point where the base turns acutely into the body of the candlestick. Make a small centre-punch mark at this point; then heat the iron round about this mark, put it vertically in

the vice with the mark just above the top edge of
the jaws and towards you, and knock over the rest
of the bar at right angles to the foot. Take the piece
from the vice, dowse it in the trough so that you may
handle it safely and with your old-fashioned tyring
wheel take from the full-size drawing the exact
length of that curve which caused you so much
trouble. You must allow extra
for the short bit immediately
below the point where the
flange is fixed. Transfer this
length to your iron, measuring
upwards from the mark and
make another centre-punch
mark. The body is now of
exactly the proper length for
bending into shape. Take it to
the anvil and lay it on the
beak; a few blows with a
hammer will give it the needful
shape and it will now look like
this sketch.

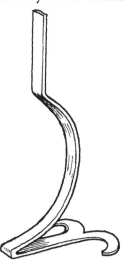

A further stage

You should now perfect the angle between the
foot and the body, so that the iron will now really
look like the beginning of a candlestick, although it
still needs the fitment for the candle.

Lay the top on the cutter and remove a little of
it; but not too much, for you have to upset it in order
to provide a decent shoulder at the root of the spill

which you next proceed to make. It is against this shoulder that the flange and socket are held firm. The spill should be about $\frac{1}{2}$ in. long and $\frac{3}{16}$ in. in diameter; and you will make matters easier for yourself if you smooth it with a running-down cutter of the appropriate size.

It is now proper to start work on the socket and flange. To make the flange you must take a piece of 20-gauge sheet iron and cut from it a disc, 3 in. in diameter. Through its centre make a $\frac{3}{16}$ in. hole and then turn a little bead round the edge of the disc. You do this quite simply in the following way.

Find an old chisel, having a $\frac{1}{2}$ in. cutting edge. Grind away the sharpness of this edge until it has become smooth and blunt. Fix the tool in the vice with the blunted edge uppermost. Lay the disc horizontally on the chisel with the circumference projecting about $\frac{1}{8}$ in. beyond the blunted edge; proceed to hammer the projecting edge from the top, when you will find that it will be turned neatly away from your hammer blows, at right angles to the rest of the disc. If you do this all the way round the circumference you will presently find that your disc has a bead around it.

Leave the tool in the vice, for you will want it again in a moment or two. The sketch shows that the disc is slightly concave from the top. You give the disc this form by resting it in a depression in a block of wood and by striking it with a ball-pane hammer. Your disc is now completed and ready for fixing. But before you can do this you must make the socket, for which you need another piece of 20-gauge iron cut in the shape of a rectangle, $3\frac{1}{2}$ in. × 2 in. Along each of the 2 in. sides, $\frac{1}{16}$ in. inwards from the edges, drill three $\frac{1}{8}$ in. holes so spaced and arranged that, when you roll the piece along its $3\frac{1}{2}$ in. sides into the form of a cylinder, the holes will coincide. Put three small rivets through the two surfaces and snap them together with a hammer, making the thing look like the upper sketch.

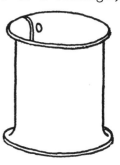

Now go back to your vice and turn a bead on the top and bottom edges of the cylinder at right angles to its walls; you know how to do this.

Finishing the socket

Cut a circular disc of a diameter $\frac{1}{8}$ in. greater than the outside diameter of the bead which you have just made on the bottom of the cylinder. Make a bead on this disc. Fit it over the bottom of the cylinder. When it is in place take hold of your hammer and, gently at first, tap the bead over and over until it tightly overlaps the turned-out edge of the bottom of the socket.

Drill a $\frac{3}{16}$ in. hole in the centre of the base of the socket; put the body of the candlestick into the vice, foot downwards; fit the flange and socket into position and satisfy yourself that they will seat firmly against the shoulder of the body where the spill projects. Then remove the body from the vice, dismantle it and get the spill white hot. Put it very quickly into the vice, drop the flange and socket into their proper position and with hammer and punch (you'll need a punch, for you can't get at the tip of the spill in any other way) rivet the end straightly and tightly.

Now you must make and fit the handle, an easy matter in itself but requiring a certain discretion in getting the curve correctly. Here again you will find that there seems to be one place—and one place only—on the sweep of the body, where that handle looks correct, with that appearance of inevitability which is to my way of thinking the hall-mark of good craftsmanship.

It is convenient to use the tyring wheel to measure off the exact length of the piece, at one of whose ends —the lower—you must forge a little spill of $\frac{3}{16}$ in. diameter. The upper end is secured to the body by a rivet. Since you know quite a lot about smithing by this time it will not be necessary for me to describe how you do this piece of fitting.

The candlestick is now almost completed; but you can spend a few minutes profitably in making an adjustment here and another there—truing-up the curve, straightening the flange and socket, making all rivet heads secure and seeing to it that the candlestick stands properly upright on its base: finally comparing it with the sketch and deciding in your own mind how far short of the full-size lay-out it has fallen. Last of all you can put it into the hands of Georgie, the apprentice, to be painted in a coat of "lead" and a couple of coats of Berlin black.

You will not be able to make a perfect candlestick at the first attempt. Your inexperience, coupled with my lame description of the process, will make that first candlestick a bit boss-eyed, probably. But go to it again. They are jolly things; and when you have finally achieved one that passes your critical eye you will feel the happier because of it.

GLOSSARY

Ball-pane hammer. A hammer with one end of the head (the "pane") shaped like half a ball. The ball-pane is used mostly for closing rivets.

Blower: Fan-blower. A device for supplying the air-blast to a forge. It is usually in the form of a circular metal casing containing a fan which is rotated at high speed by suitably geared hand or mechanical power.

Blue-print. A copy of a drawing made from a tracing by a simple photographic printing method, and very largely used in engineering. The ground colour of the finished print is bright blue, the lines of the drawing being white.

Centre-punch. A small steel punch with a sharp conical point. It is used to make a tiny V-shaped depression in a piece of metal, either as a mark or in order to start the point of a drill.

Clip. In decorative wrought-iron work, a small strip of iron bent round two adjacent scrolls or parts of a grille in order to hold them together.

Drilling. The method of boring a hole in metal by using a rotating "drill-bit" which cuts away the metal as it turns. The drill-bit may be used in a "drill-brace", which is turned by hand, or in a drilling-machine, worked by hand or mechanical power.

Hacksawing. Cutting through metal by means of a specially hardened steel saw, which has usually a narrow blade held in tension in a frame.

Jig. A device used in repetition work, especially in machine methods of production, whereby the cutting tool is guided into the same position when operating in succession on a large number of similar pieces of material. Each operation needs to have a jig specially made for it.

Monkey tool. A hollow cylindrical tool with a flat end, used for shaping the shoulder of a "spill" (q.v.). The monkey tool is placed over the spill and hammered down on to the shoulder, thus accurately flattening it in a position which could not easily be reached by the hammer.

Overthrow of gate. The decorative ironwork placed above the top bar of a gate.

Riveting. The method of binding together two or more pieces of metal with a pin, usually of the same metal. The pin is provided with a ready-made head at one end. When the rivet has been put in position the other end is spread out ("snapped over") with a ball-pane hammer.

Running-down cutter. A tool used in the drill-brace to trim a spill after it has been forged by means of a monkey tool (q.v.). The hollow cylindrical cutter is placed over the spill and rotated, when its cutting edges remove any inaccuracies there may be in the spill and the shoulder.

Scale. The layer of hard black oxide formed on the surface of iron when it is heated in the forge fire.

Sledge-hammer. A large heavy hammer, used in two hands, and often swung over the head when striking.

Soldering. A method of joining metals in which an alloy ("solder"), more fusible than the metals to be joined, is used to unite them. A suitable "flux" has to be applied to prevent the oxidisation of the surfaces to be joined, and the solder is melted either by the application of a heated "soldering-bit" or by a blowpipe.

Spill: Spilled end. A cylindrical peg formed on the end of a metal bar. (See illustration on p. 39.) The flat end of the bar round the base of the spill is known as the "shoulder".

Template. A specially made pattern or gauge used to guide the marking-out or cutting tool when a process has to be repeated a number of times on successive pieces of material.

Tue iron. The iron nozzle through which the air-blast emerges into the forge fire. As it is surrounded by the glowing coals, the tue iron gets very hot. In modern forges its temperature is kept down by a system of water circulation. The name comes from the French *tuyère*, which term is sometimes used in this country.

Tyring wheel. A disc of metal a few inches in diameter, fixed in a handle so that it can rotate as its edge is run along a curved line. Its use is described on p. 82.

INDEX

For EU product safety concerns, contact us at Calle de José Abascal, 56–1°,
28003 Madrid, Spain or eugpsr@cambridge.org.

www.ingramcontent.com/pod-product-compliance
Ingram Content Group UK Ltd.
Pitfield, Milton Keynes, MK11 3LW, UK
UKHW012334130625
459647UK00009B/282